CHOREOGRAPHY & STYLE FOR ICE SKATERS

CHOREOGRAPHY & STYLE FOR ICE SKATERS

RICKY HARRIS

ILLUSTRATIONS BY JERRY SCHWARTZ

ST. MARTIN'S PRESS NEW YORK

Library of Congress Cataloging-in-Publication Data

Harris, Ricky.
    Choreography & style for ice skaters / Ricky Harris.
      p.   cm.
    Includes index.
    ISBN 0-312-05401-7
    1. Skating. 2. Choreography. I. Title. II. Title: Choreography
and style for ice skaters.
    GV850.4.H37 1991   90-19105
    796.91′2—dc20   CIP

First U.S. Paperback Edition
10 9 8 7 6 5 4 3 2 1

This book is respectfully and affectionately dedicated to Eugene Loring—dancer, choreographer, and educator—whose knowledge and ideas have been the inspiration for this book.

CONTENTS

FOREWORD
ACKNOWLEDGMENTS
INTRODUCTION

PART ONE
ELEMENTS OF CHOREOGRAPHY

PART TWO
CREATING A SKATING PROGRAM

PART THREE
ADDITIONAL TRAINING ASPECTS

FOREWORD

The dream of every skater is to give a truly great performance—one that he knows, and that the judges and audience know, has been a perfect combination of strength, technique, and artistry—a perfect matching of skater to music to movement.

Such performances may seem effortless and inspired, but this is usually far from the case. A skater must practice endless hours on such things as timing, positioning, facial expression, gesture, and footwork. But, more important, he must learn to be aware of his own abilities and limitations as a skater. He must experiment with new ways to communicate his feelings and emotions, and explore new types of music and movement that best suit his style.

To us, being creative doesn't mean being the first to use a new spin or movement. To us, creativity means the ability to perform any movement—new or old—in a style that is truly your own—that matches your body, and personality and abilities. And we feel it's this kind of creativity and style that makes a skater stand out as unique on the ice.

We've been lucky that our coach, John Nicks, is a believer in creative freedom. He hasn't forced us to imitate a certain style just because it's classic or because it's worked for skaters in the past. He's encouraged us to study ballet and jazz and to be creative in developing our own style.

Ricky Harris is a believer, too. A passionate believer. And she has very carefully and very intelligently taken a difficult subject and put it down on paper so that it makes sense.

Choreography and Style for Ice Skaters is a book that we've needed for a long long time. It's the first book we know of that explains —in a logical way—how to go about choosing music and choreographing a routine from beginning to end. But the book goes beyond the basics, because Ricky doesn't believe in choosing just any music or just any way of skating to it. She explains how to study your own personality and abilities and to choose the music and movements that are right for *you*. She also gives innovative training techniques on how to focus energy, how to improvise, and how to experiment with gestures and movement.

This is a fun book, but also an informative book that should be of help to skaters of all levels—both professional and amateur. It's a book we wish we'd had when we started skating pairs a decade ago.

—Tai Babilonia
—Randy Gardner

ACKNOWLEDGMENTS

For the sanction of all photographs of their registered amateur members, I wish to acknowledge the United States Figure Skating Association.

To Louella and Jerry Rehfield and Shiela Turek, my warmest thanks for their suggestions on several chapters.

I am sincerely grateful to Joe Marshall for his special help and great sense of humor.

For his valuable contributions to the chapter on "Warming Up," I wish to express my appreciation to Anatol Podolsky.

I wish to acknowledge all of the world-class skaters whose photographs appear in this book. That their photographs appear does not necessarily mean that they endorse the book or its methods; I have included their photographs because they demonstrate good and effective use of style on the ice. These skaters are: Toller Cranston, John Curry, Denise Biellmann, Peggy Fleming, Maia Usova, Alexander Zhulin, Viktor Petrenko, Scott Hamilton, Katarina Witt, Doug Williams, Sharon Carz, Jill Trenary, Marina Khimova, Sergei Ponomarenko, Christopher Dean, Jane Torvill, Janet Lynn, Belita, Ekaterina Gordeeva, Sergei Grinkov, Brian Boitano, Irina Moiseeva, Andrei Minenkov, Tai Babilonia, Randy Gardner, Sonja Henie, Charles Tickner, and Wendy Burge. Also, my thanks to the photographer, identity unknown, of the Sonja Henie photograph.

My love and appreciation go to my son, John, who offered many suggestions "on the run;" and to my daughter, Hillary, who spent numerous hours reading the manuscript and proposing valuable suggestions and corrections.

And most of all, to Paul, who encouraged me to finally start the manuscript, gave me the "space" I needed to accomplish it, fed me when I forgot to eat, comforted me when I became discouraged, and surrounded me with his devotion; I give my fervent gratitude and love.

INTRODUCTION

While traveling around the United States conducting my Creative Choreographic Workshops for ice skaters, I had many requests for some sort of written material compiling the Workshop theories and exercises. This book has been written in answer to those requests.

The Creative Choreographic Workshop presents ideas on how to improve composition and style. It teaches basic concepts of choreography which can be applied to ice skating. The Workshop exercises are for every skater in singles, pairs, or dance, either amateur or professional, and lead to the awakening of creativity and the development of a personal style of skating. These workshop concepts will be presented in the following pages.

For many years competitive ice skating has been an athletic event, a technique, an acrobatic spectacle. Since it has moved in the direction of also becoming an art form, stylistic approach has become an important concern. In amateur competitions, one set of marks is given for the technical merit of the skater's program. This includes spins, jumps, and footwork. The other set of marks is for composition and style, which judges the artistic side of the program.

In the *Oxford English Dictionary*, the definition of composition is:

1. The action of combining; the fact of being combined; combination of (parts of elements of a whole).

2. The forming (of anything) by combination of parts, etc; formation, construction.

3. Orderly arrangement; ordering.

Style in ice skating is the presence and manner in which the skater performs an action, his carriage and bearing, and the effect and impression he leaves on the viewer. *The United States Figure Skating Association Rulebook* states:

323. In the marking of composition and style, the following must be considered:
    (a) harmonious composition of the program as a whole and its conformity to the music chosen;
    (b) utilization of space;
    (c) easy movement and sureness in time to the music;
    (d) carriage;
    (e) originality;
    (f) expression of the character of music.

In dance, choreography is influenced by motivation and musical inspiration. The choreographer and dancers are not trying to win a competition, so there is much more freedom and license in the creative process. There are no time limits, so each dance work lasts as long as needed to fulfill the ideas and motivation of the choreographer. A dance work could be three minutes or it could be an hour. Choreography for competitive skating necessitates a different approach, as competitive rules must be followed.

Communication through dance is a vital force which has affected the colorful and exciting sport of ice skating, making competition not only a contest filled with uncertainty, supreme endeavors, defeated expectations, and glory; but also a colorful drama with very defined roles.

Each person has an individual way of moving which becomes

a part of his or her personality and uniqueness of communication. It is my purpose in this book to help you to appreciate your uniqueness and discover the differences between yourself and other skaters through self-awareness and self-analysis.

On the following pages you will find collective processes which will help you to understand your body's potential. The exercises will guide you toward the development of a personal style and greater self-responsibility. They will stimulate you to new creative approaches toward choreography and the achievement of your goals.

I feel a mixture of emotions at finishing this book. There is a tremendous relief at its completion. Now, at last, I can give my mind a rest. I will not wake up at all hours of the night to sit at my desk, trying to verbalize my thoughts, But there is also a feeling of emptiness that surrounds me; for this book has filled my thoughts, day and night, since I began writing it. It is my hope that it will occupy a portion of your life, and bring new joy and creativity to your skating career.

PART ONE

ELEMENTS OF CHOREOGRAPHY

Chapter 1
ENERGIZE
AND
IMPROVISE

If I were a heathen, I would rear a statue to energy and fall down and worship it.

—Mark Twain

Stand up!

1. Pull your stomach in until it feels as if it is pushing against your spine.

2. Keeping your stomach pulled in, lift your chest.

3. Squeeze your buttocks together.

4. Press down with your shoulders and back muscles.

5. Lift your chin.

6. Raise your arms until they reach the level of your shoulders.

7. Stretch your fingers and imagine your fingertips trying to touch the walls on each side of you.

These seven steps comprise the IES—Isometric Energy Stretch.

n the ten seconds that it takes you to accomplish the above seven steps, you will feel a tremendous stretch and surge of energy throughout your entire body.

You have your own source of energy inside your body, the

extent of which is determined by proper exercise, diet, and mental attitudes. Energy is force put to work. The more force put to work, the more energy is supplied.

Our potential energy supply is much greater than we suspect. Many people go through life tapping only a small percentage of it. There is a large source of energy in the magnetic fields that surround our bodies, moving about in electrical currents. Through experimentation and practice, you can become like a magnet, attracting this potential energy from the currents around you and connecting them to the energy within your body. It is like the electricity in a room. When a switch is turned on, energy is produced in the form of light. Finding the "switch" in the body and "turning it on" to produce energy will make you a more exciting performer.

Perform the seven basic steps of the IES with the following focal points:

IES **1.** Using your arms and hands as your focal points, imagine that they do not end at the fingertips, but extend into space. With this thought you will find a new vitality in the arms and hands as they try to reach the source of the energy field.

IES **2.** Imagine the top of your head pulling up, trying to reach the ceiling.

IES **3.** Feel as if the muscles in the top part of the back are squeezing together and pulling toward a point in the center of the back.

IES **4.** Push your belly button back toward your spine.

IES **5.** Squeeze your buttocks together.

IES **6.** Try to feel the muscles in your legs lengthening. Imagine the tops of the thighs ending at the waist.

IES **7.** Keeping your back upright so that it is in a vertical line with your feet, raise one leg backward. Stretch the leg and point the toes, trying to reach away from the body toward the back wall of the room. Make sure the knees are perfectly straight and the thigh muscles are pulled up. If you are not sure they are straight, bend the knees and then straighten them again. Reverse legs and repeat. (See Fig. 1.)

Hold each step for ten counts.

Repeat each step four times.

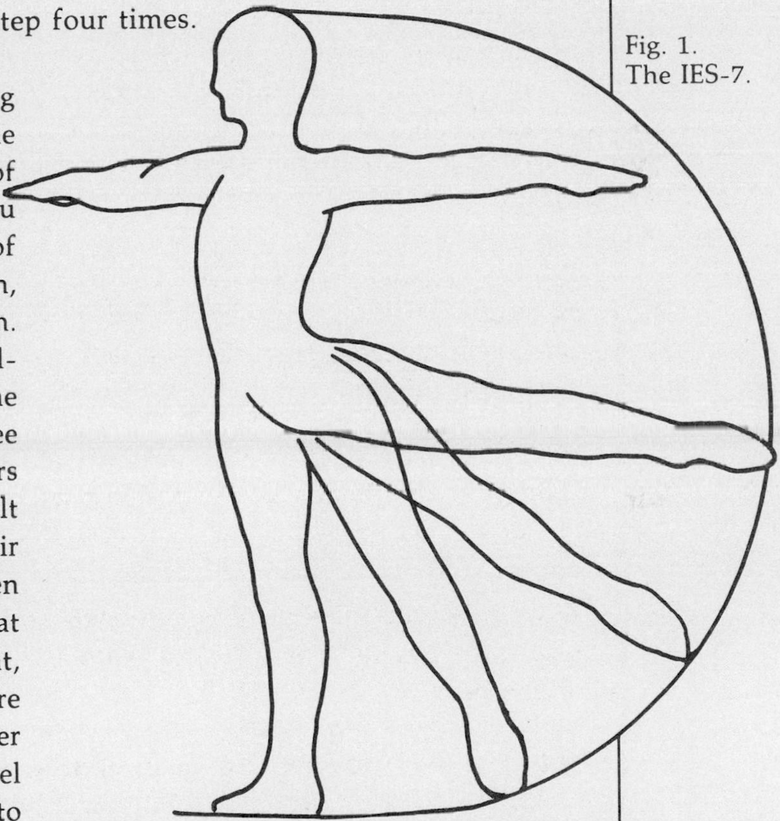

By applying the IES to the different parts of the body, you will gain a look of strength, stretch, and expression. This is especially helpful in the use of the free leg. Many skaters find it difficult to stretch their free leg. When they are told that their leg is bent, they usually are surprised. After learning to feel the stretch into the energy field outside the body, they soon recognize the feeling of the completely extended leg.

Fig. 1.
The IES-7.

Now that you have experienced the IES exercises on the floor, start incorporating them into your daily work on the ice. Start with some basic stroking around the rink and go through the IES–1 through 6 around the curves of the rink's oval; and the IES–7 along the long narrow sides, using inside edges and alternating feet. (See Fig. 2). Repeat all the exercises, stroking in the reverse direction.

Fig. 2.

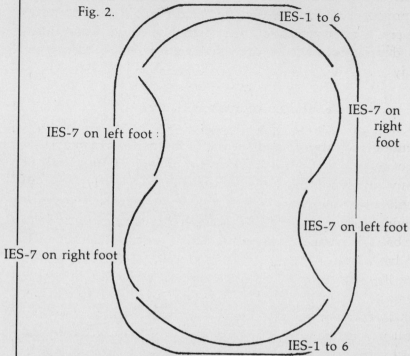

IES-1 to 6

IES-7 on right foot

IES-7 on left foot :

IES-7 on left foot

IES-7 on right foot

IES-1 to 6

Exercises using the theory of energy in and around the body not only develop higher levels of energy in the slow sections and energetic sharpness in the fast sections of a skating program, but also teach the art of improvisation.

Improvisation in skating and dance is movement performed without plan or rehearsal. It is an important tool needed for originating movement by both the amateur and the professional. Improvisation is not the same as creating specific movements. The ability to improvise easily and fluently is a valuable preliminary to choreography. Choreography is deliberately creating movements that have content, form, design in space and time, dynamics, rhythm, and motivation.

The concentration of moving an imagined "energy ball" to different parts of your body will help you to move in ways that you may not have imagined before. You will be able to create original moves because you are using a unique instrument, your own body.

At first you may find it difficult to begin the process of improvisation. Within a short time, as the following exercises are practiced, improvising will become a resourceful method in the development of a personal style, and will help make your body/instrument a sensitive and creative source.

SINGLE ENERGY BALL FLOW

To start the process of improvising movement with the expenditure of energy, stand in front of a mirror and imagine that all of the energy in and around your body is compressed into a tiny energy ball that rests in the center of the body. You will begin to move the energy ball slowly through the body with flowing control, making sure that you can see and feel where the ball is at all times. The ball must move successively through the body, just as blood flows through the veins. This means that if you are trying to move the ball from the pit of the stomach to the right shoulder, you must be able to see and feel it move through the chest, neck, and out to the right shoulder. As it moves out of the stomach and into the chest area, the chest should lift as a result of the concentration of energy in that section. This will also apply to the neck, which will stretch up as the ball reaches it. When the ball moves into the right shoulder region, the shoulder will also rise so that you can see where the energy is. Successive movements are those that pass through the body in succession like a ripple, moving each joint and muscle as you come to it. The movements are wavelike and fluid. These successive movements will create an even flow of energy, controlled by you.

To move the energy ball to the right knee:
> Ball moves from stomach. . . .
>> to right hip
>> to right thigh
>> to right knee.

To move the energy ball to the left hip:
> Ball moves from right knee. . . .

to right thigh
to right hip
to stomach
to left hip (see Fig. 3).

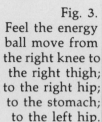

Fig. 3.
Feel the energy
ball move from
the right knee to
the right thigh;
to the right hip;
to the stomach;
to the left hip.

To move the energy ball to the fingers of your left hand, out into space, and back to your stomach:

Ball moves from left hip. . . .
        to left waist
        to left rib cage
        to left shoulder
        to left upper arm
        to left elbow
        to left lower arm
        to left wrist
        to back of left hand
        to left fingers
        out into space
        back into left fingers
        to back of left hand
        to left wrist
        to left lower arm
        to left elbow
        to left upper arm
        to left shoulder
        to neck
        to chest
        to waist
        to stomach.

Although upper arm movements are guided by the elbow and the lower arm is carried along, thinking of the energy ball in this order will help attain a flow. Make sure the energy ball is in only one place at a time, and that all other parts of the body are relaxed.

The torso is the source and main instrument of true emotional expression. Successions are used to display this expression through the body flow. Therefore, successions, learned by using energy balls, begin in the torso and spread outward and downward throughout the entire body.

It is time for *you* to instruct yourself as to where the energy ball will go. Put on some music and then concentrate on moving the energy ball to all the different parts of your body.

Make the ball:

wiggle your nose
roll your eyes
pull you to the floor
curl your toes
round your back
flex your foot
flex your hand . . .

. . . and anything else you can think of. When you have practiced the Single Energy Ball Flow enough to be able to see the ball flowing to all parts of the body, you will be ready to try it on the ice. You may practice by yourself, or find a partner to work with you and take turns instructing where the ball should go. The instructor can let the partner know if the energy can really be seen in the part of the body where the ball has moved.

Be daring! Go all out! Really move that ball and let it move you on the ice. Let yourself fall into three turns, mohawks, and footwork by the strength of the energy ball moving. Don't try to make pretty or handsome movements. Just let it happen! The body will automatically fall into certain postures. Remember, you are not trying to choreograph or invent any movements at this point. You are merely experimenting with moving energy around in your body.

Don't rush in your practice of the Single Energy Ball Flow. Practice it over and over until you become confident of the way the energy is progressing through your body.

DOUBLE ENERGY BALL FLOW

When you feel ready, you may try to use two energy balls flowing through the body together. Go back to working on the floor in front of a mirror. Watch to see that you are moving only two balls at a time. This will take discipline and control. Your movement forms are now taking on a different look, a two-dimensional one.

When you have captured the idea of the two energy balls, you will want to try it on the ice. Now there will be so many more ways your body will move. Take your time; there are no shortcuts to developing your new image, your new style. Treat these exercises as you would school figures. You will want to repeat them over daily and improve—improve—improve.

ENERGY BALL ISOLATIONS

Because not all music you skate to is slow and flowing, you will also want to express energy in the body in a quick and marked manner. You can accomplish this by letting the energy ball jump from one place in the body to another.

> Snap the energy ball
> > from the stomach . . .
> > to the right hip
> > to the left elbow
> > to the right knee
> > to the top of the head
> > to the left foot
> > to the left knee turned in
> > to the left knee turned out
> > to the right shoulder
> > to the stomach.

You can have fun with Energy Ball Isolations. Move them fast. Direct yourself where to snap the ball and then try it on the ice with any fast music being played. It will make your movements hop, jump, push, pull, contract, bend, and twist.

MULTIPLE ENERGY BALLS

It is now time to let out all barriers and allow the energy to flow and snap through your entire body, using as many energy balls as you like. You will sense an immediate feeling of release as your body begins moving in a multitude of ways, and you can let it happen without trying to discipline the action in one or

two places. At
first you may
look like a
Raggedy Ann or
Andy as you
bend and twist,
stretch and ex-
tend. You will
feel marvelous at
being able to ex-
press energy in
parts of your
body that were
static and dull
before.

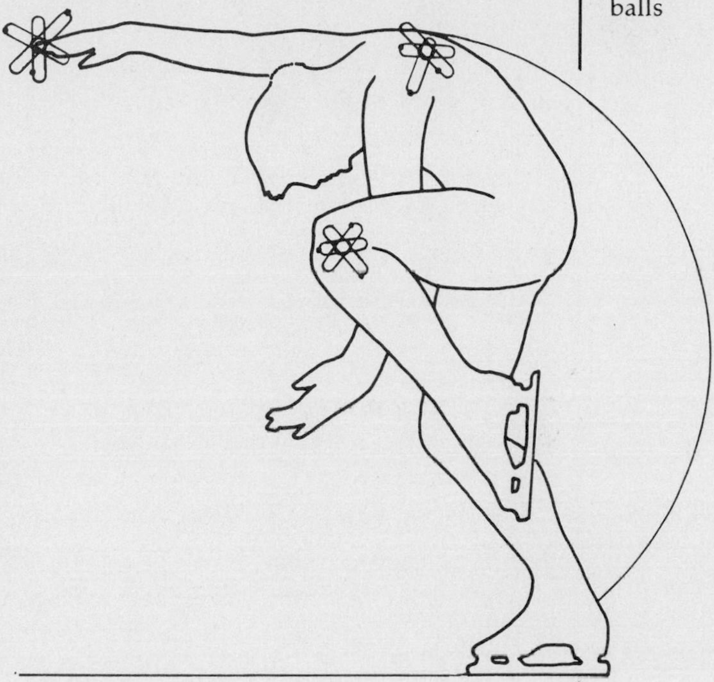

Of course you
would not want
to do a whole
program with
multiple energy
balls! But you
now have a tool

Fig. 4.
Multiple
energy
balls

that you can use not only to put expression in your body, but
also to invent new movement forms.

It is a good idea to practice the energy exercises daily. Schedule a certain amount of time daily for choreography and style
practice. It might be ten or fifteen minutes of every freestyle.
As you move the energy balls, be aware of the music that is
playing in the rink. Try to move the energy balls to flow with
it. As the different programs are played, change the way the
energy balls move to match the music. How exciting it will be
to discover yourself moving in new ways. You are now at the
beginning of developing your own personal style!

Chapter 2

MUSIC FOR SKATERS

Music is more than black notes on white paper. It's what is in between that counts.

—Zubin Mehta

A simple understanding of the basics of written music will help you to understand rhythmic changes in your program music, and open your mind to the subtleties of movement that can best interpret your music. When listening to music, you will be able to determine the various dynamics and qualities that can be transferred to your skating. Being aware of rhythmic qualities and fulfilling musical values in your choreography will help you to achieve an artistic awareness that will make you an exciting musical performer.

For many years music was used merely as a background for a skater's program. There was a time when skaters who tried to be original and perform creative programs were criticized and even marked down for their attempts when judged competitively. As skaters learned more of ballet, modern dance, and jazz, they became unsatisfied with a purely athletic type of program. Some began to skate beautiful programs expressing their music.

Unfortunately, not everyone is born with a sense of timing and rhythm. I have seen excellent skaters who have difficulty keeping time to music and do not seem able to hear downbeats and phrases. These people have to be taught, and with persistence they can learn. One of the most creative choreographers I know, who is now the chairman of a dance department at a

Midwestern college, had this difficulty when she was my classmate in the dance department of the university I attended. Through consistent study and work, she learned; and she is successful in her field today.

Musical training is an important aspect in the development of a sensitive and expressive skater. Knowing basic note values, how to count music, how music is phrased, and being able to coordinate it with movement phrases, make a wide difference in a program, and have a dramatic effect on the composition and style of the performing skater.

I do not believe it is mandatory for you to learn how to play a musical instrument, although it could be advantageous. Understanding written music can help in your musical appreciation, making it easier to select music for programs. In conducting workshops throughout the United States I have found that even skaters who are accomplished musicians do not always "connect" the musical directions of dynamics and articulations to their skating programs. Though you may be a musician, it would be beneficial for you to study all the material in this chapter, and follow each exercise through to its completion.

NOTE VALUES

All music is written on a staff which consists of five horizontal lines. The staff is broken up into vertical lines called bar lines, which separate the music into sections called measures (see Fig. 5 below). Sometimes measures are referred to as bars.

Fig. 5.

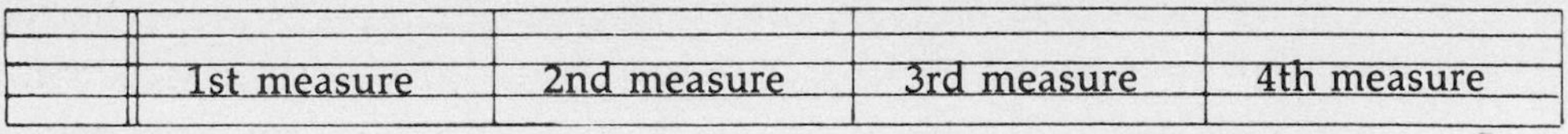

| 1st measure | 2nd measure | 3rd measure | 4th measure |

Musical notes show how long to hold a sound (see Figs. 6 and 7).

Fig. 6.

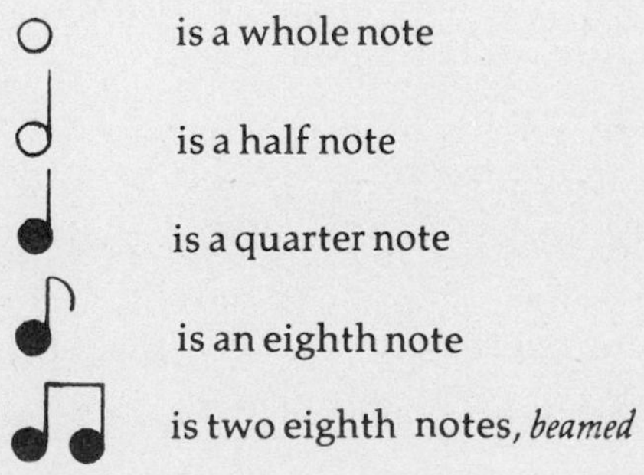

○　is a whole note

○̣　is a half note

●　is a quarter note

♪　is an eighth note

♫　is two eighth notes, *beamed*

−11−

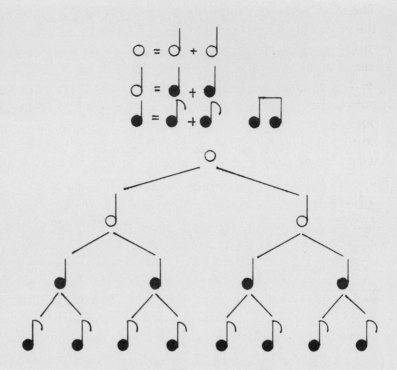

One whole note equals two half notes
One half note equals two quarter notes
One quarter note equals two eighth notes

Music has a basic beat (count). In most music this basic beat is represented by the quarter note. When the quarter note gets one count it affects other note values (see Fig. 7).

Fig. 7.

♩ = quarter note, gets 1 count

♩ = half note, gets 2 counts

𝅝 = whole note, gets 4 counts

♪ = eighth note, gets ½ count

♫ = two eighth notes, get 1 count

Before music is written, the time signature must be determined. For the purposes of this book, only two time signatures will be discussed:

4 means   four counts to each measure (meter) (see Fig. 8a)
4 means   quarter note gets one count

3 means   three counts to each measure (meter) (see Fig. 8b)
4 means   quarter note gets one count

The time signature is always written next to the music clef at the beginning of the staff (see Fig. 8). There are two numbers involved in the time signature. The top number signifies the meter. The meter tells how many counts will be in each measure. The bottom number signifies what note gets one count:
If bottom note is 4, then the quarter note gets one count.
If bottom note is 2, then the half note gets one count.
If bottom note is 8, then the eighth note gets one count.
Since the quarter note value of one count is the most common, this is the only one that will be used in the exercises.

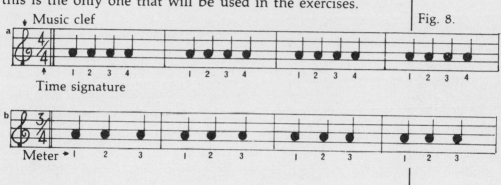

Fig. 8.

DIVISION OF METER IS RHYTHM

Within each measure, the meter can be broken up with different note values according to the desire of the composer, so long as they add up to the count of the stated meter. This is called rhythm. You will be translating rhythm into physical actions, so it is important to know counts in order to know on which count an action must come.

Fig. 9.

Each single count is numbered according to where it is in the measure. In Fig. 9, looking at the numbers on the top of the staff signifying the rhythm, you will find that the first measure contains four quarter notes and that they are numbered consecutively 1,2,3,4. In the second measure, the first note is called 1; the second is called 2; and the third note (half note) is called

3,4. Each note must be held in accordance with its given time value. When the quarter note is divided in half, the first eighth note is called 1, and the second eighth note is called *and,* as in measures 3 and 4 of Fig. 10.

Fig. 10.

In Fig. 9 there are four counts in the last measure although there is only one note. That is because it is a whole note and worth four counts. In the third measure there are only two notes, but the measure is still worth four counts as each half note is worth two counts. In 3/4 time you cannot use whole notes, as that would give you four counts in one measure.

Look at Fig. 10. Count out the notes in each measure. If you clap your hands to the rhythm of the first measure, you would clap once and hold it for two counts; then clap one more time, holding it for one count. You have three even claps in the second measure. In the third measure, you would clap four times, but the two middle eighth notes would have claps twice as fast as the first and last quarter note claps.

In the last measure of Fig. 10 you would clap six times. Each note in the measure gets a clap, but the claps are held half as long as the quarter note claps.

A good way to practice until you understand the rhythm is to work with a partner. Have your partner clap the meter of the Fig. 9 staff. This means your partner will be clapping four counts for each measure, with no time break between measures. At the same time, you will clap the rhythm. Notice in the last measure that you begin at the same time with 1, but you keep silent for 2,3,4, while your partner claps 2,3,4.

When you are satisfied that your rhythm is correct for Fig. 9, work on Fig. 10 and Fig. 11 in the same manner.

Fig. 11.

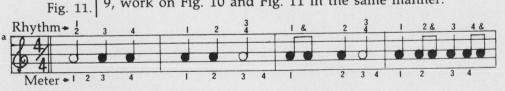

FINDING YOUR PROGRAM METER

To determine the meter of your program music, first listen carefully to the record or tape and try to tap out the beat or pulse of the music with your foot. Work with a very small section at a time, and play it over and over until you can hear the beat.

Now listen for any accents in the music. An accent is one note that is louder than the others, or perhaps higher than the others. Tap the accents louder than the other beats and pay attention to how often they occur. If they are on every second note, the music would be in 2/2, 2/4, or 2/8 time (two counts to a measure). If the accents are on every third beat, the music would be in 3/2, 3/4, or 3/8 time (three counts to a measure). If the accents are repeated every fourth beat, then the music is in 4/2, 4/4, or 4/8 time (four counts to a measure). There are other, more complicated time signatures that, for the purposes of this book, need not be discussed. In Fig. 12 the strong accents are marked with >.

Fig. 12.

DOWNBEATS AND UPBEATS

The first beat of the measure is called the downbeat. The last beat of the measure is called the upbeat. In musical circles the upbeat is sometimes referred to as a pickup. Upbeats and

-15-

downbeats relate to the way a conductor moves his baton in space. The first beat of the measure is indicated by a downward gesture, and the last by an upward gesture. You should be able to recognize the downbeat as you might have to start moving on the first beat of the music, or perform a strong movement on the downbeat of a measure.

The purpose of the upbeat is to prepare for the downbeat. Some music starts on an upbeat. When this happens the upbeat is written before the first bar line and is not counted with the first measure. An example of this is the Christmas song "Away in the Manger" (see Fig. 13).

Fig. 13.

Many ice programs are difficult to count musically. With the knowledge gained in this chapter and the counting expertise you will acquire from practicing the exercises, you should be able to get an approximate count of your music. Remember that you will be moving in *relationship* with your music, rather than always moving to the music itself.

If you have difficulty understanding the exercises immediately, do not be discouraged. It takes time and repeated explanations to comprehend music theory. Do not hesitate to go back to the beginning of the chapter and move at your own speed. Read each explanation over and do the exercises only after thoroughly understanding them.

Rhythm Exercise 1

1. Go over Figs. 9 through 12. This time work by yourself. Insert the accents in Figs. 9 through 11.

2. Clap the rhythm (every note you see), holding each note for its time value.

3. Keep the meter with your feet by walking in place.

4. Bend your knee on the downbeats. (See Fig. 12.)

Rhythm Exercise 2

1. Compose two staffs of music made up of four measures each in 3/4 time, using half notes, quarter notes, and eighth notes. Each measure should be different.

2. Clap out the rhythm of each measure until you do it well.

3. Standing, keep time to the meter with your feet, stepping right and left alternately, using kneebends for the downbeats.

4. Combine the rhythm and meter by clapping and stepping together.

Rhythm Exercise 3

1. Compose two staffs made up of four measures each in 4/4 time and proceed as in Exercise 2. Include whole notes in your music.

2. Walk around the room as you step the meter.

Rhythm Exercise 4

1. Select one of the staffs you have composed. Create an arm movement that will replace each clap and last only as long as the clap. Remember that the arm movement must be moving for the full length of the note value. For example, in Fig. 11a, the first note is a half note and holds for two counts. Your arm movement then must keep moving for two counts. The second arm movement will last one count, and your third arm movement will last one count. Keep the arm movements very simple so you can concentrate on following the rhythmic pattern.

2. After memorizing the arm movements for the first measure, walk the meter and do the arm movements to the rhythm at the same time. When you have accomplished this, go on to the next measure until you get through the entire staff.

3. Work all four of your compositions in this manner.

DYNAMICS

Dynamics in music signifies the different levels in the volume of sound; the varying degrees of loudness and softness. Music is rarely played at one dynamic level; it would be uninteresting. There should be a sense of dynamics in skating also, where you feel the music and the movement as one. Musical dynamics are indicated by special words or symbols:

	Italian	Symbol
very soft	pianissimo	pp
soft	piano	p
moderately soft	mezzo piano	mp
moderately loud	mezzo forte	mf
loud	forte	f
very loud	fortissimo	ff

Dynamics in music is the amount of power in sound: loud or soft. Dynamics in skating is the amount of effort put into the movement.

You can find many fine distinctions in movement just by studying the two dynamics of *forte* and *piano.*

Forte

Forte Exercise 1. To get the feeling of moving in *forte,* picture yourself covered to the neck in a vat of peanut butter! Really feel the peanut butter all around you. Try to remember how it feels when you put a spoonful of peanut butter in your mouth and try to move your tongue around and through it. Move your arms with a lot of effort through this imaginary peanut butter mass.

Forte Exercise 2. Experiment with moving an energy ball

through your body while it is encased in an imaginary tunnel of molasses. Make the energy ball go to every part of your body, using a lot of effort to make the ball move from one place to another. First use a single energy ball, then double energy balls. Use lots of tension.

Forte Exercise 3. Use the Energy Ball Isolation Exercise (see chapter 1) to make *forte* movements happen in quicker time. Make sure

Fig. 14.
Moving with effort *(forte)* through an imaginary peanut butter mass.

that you are still putting a lot of effort behind each movement, even though it is not a slow, flowing movement.

Forte Exercise 4. Take two of the musical staffs you composed and perform them with the arm movements in *forte*.

Piano

Piano Exercise 1. To get a feeling of moving in *piano*, picture yourself in a vat of whipped cream. It is so easy to move the different parts of your body through the imaginary fluffs of whipped cream. Let your body swirl and wiggle, feeling the cream all around you.

Piano Exercise 2. Move single and double energy balls through tunnels of imaginary foam, making soft, "no effort" movements.

Piano Exercise 3. Use the Energy Ball Isolation Exercise to make *piano* movements happen in quicker time.

Piano Exercise 4. Take your remaining two compositions and perform the arm movements in *piano.*

Music will tell you the *forte* and *piano* by how loud and soft it is. Experiment with different moods by using these dynamics to direct your movements. Becoming aware of *piano* and *forte* dynamics in movement can color your program with character, variety, and expression.

ARTICULATION

Different expressive qualities can be attained in music by the way in which notes are performed. This is called articulation. There are three basic types of articulation: marcato, legato, and staccato.

Marcato

Notes played in marcato are clearly defined and marked. They have a marchlike quality to them, a driving force behind them. One example of marcato is the "Jets Song" from *West Side Story.* When you sing the scale—Do Re Mi, etc.—you are singing in marcato.

Legato

The term legato signifies connected notes; notes that are like a slur where you hardly hear an attack. These notes are tied together without a pause. Most of the music used for the slow parts of your program is played in legato. You would not be able to hear a marked beginning or end of these notes as they are connected to each other. "The Impossible Dream" from the musical play *Man of La Mancha* is an example of a song in legato.

Staccato

In staccato each note is separated. Each note is played with an attack that is touched and quickly taken away. It is like a quick action separated in time from the next. Beethoven's Fifth Symphony is a good example of staccato, as well as Walter Murphy's disco version of it, "Fifth of Beethoven."

Articulation Exercise 1. Using your staff compositions, practice the arm movements first in marcato, then in legato, and finally in staccato. You may have to change the arm movements slightly to conform to the different articulations. Your arm movements in legato would follow one another very smoothly without a break. You would not be able to see the beginning or end of each movement as they would be blended together. In marcato and staccato arm movements, try to clearly see the beginning and ending of each move. Your staccato moves would be shorter than the marcato moves.

Articulation Exercise 2. Vary the articulations in each staff, using marcato for one measure, legato for another, and staccato for another. Go through your staff compositions and write the articulations in each measure and then perform the arm movements according to your directions.

Over a period of repetitive practice, these music exercises will help you to keep time and extend the music; which is one of the more important aspects of expressive skating. Extending the music results in a beautiful flow. Your interpretation of the music articulations with your body will help you to develop your individual style, as you explore new relationships between movement and music, and find new dimensions in your skating.

Chapter 3

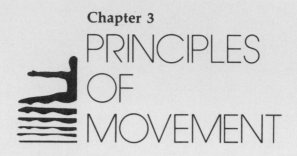

PRINCIPLES OF MOVEMENT

When people are free to do as they please, they usually imitate each other.

—Eric Hoffer

By this time you have learned several ways to invent simple movements through the process of improvisation and interpreting musical directions. Working with the dynamics and articulations of your music has helped you to experience some degree of feeling and expression.

ELEMENTS OF MOVEMENT

When you understand the theory of movement, you no longer have to imitate. Instead, you can create your own style. With this thought in mind, you are now ready to investigate different types of movement that will provide you with another tool in the choreographic process. There are many ways your body can move.

Ascending	Twisting	Bouncing
Descending	Rolling	Running
Falling	Darting	Shaking
Bending	Jumping	Swinging
Extending	Pulling	Pushing
Turning		

It is important that you do not limit yourself to accomplishing each element with just one part of your body. Think of how many joints in your body can change to make these movements occur. You will find that some of the descriptions of the elements overlap, but there are enough differences to allow for purposeful movements.

Ascending

An ascending movement is made by any part of your body rising with control or resistance from a lowered position.

1. Ascend with your arm, one shoulder, a knee, one hip, your head, a leg.

2. Start on the floor and ascend with your entire body up to a kneeling or standing position.

Descending

Descending is the opposite of ascending. The movement starts from a raised position and lowers with resistance or control.

1. Descend with the separate parts of your body.

2. Descend with the whole body as a unit.

Falling

Having the whole or parts of your body lower with the pull of gravity is falling. Once falling has begun, you should have the feeling that the action cannot be stopped. The difference between falling and descending is that descending is moving down with control, and falling is moving down without control. Do not limit yourself by thinking of a fall as the whole body falling to the floor.

1. With a raised arm, let it "fall" by dropping it to your side without control.

2. Lift your head to an upright position and let it "fall" to your chest.

3. Make your shoulder "fall" by having it collapse or slump to the side.

Bending

Bending is curving away from a straight line.

1. Bend forward, backward, and to the side from your chest area; from your hip area.

2. Bend your arms and legs at the elbows and knees.

3. Flex your feet and hands by bending your ankles and wrists.

4. Bend your head in any direction.

Extending (Stretching)

Extending is lengthening any part of the body into a particular direction. To experience extension, do the following:

1. Double your body over and slowly straighten it.

2. Bend your knee and proceed to straighten your leg completely.

3. Bend your elbow, then lengthen your arm to its fullest.

Turning (Rotation)

Turning is a partial or complete rotating motion around an axis or a center. It is also a movement that changes its direction by facing another way.

1. Turn your head from side to side.

2. Turn your body partially or around in a complete circle.

3. With your arms out, palms up, turn the palms down.

Twisting (Rotation)

Parts of the body both rotate and twist. Twisting occurs when a free end is able to rotate farther than its base. Twisting is rotating against resistance.

1. Holding one arm out in front of you, twist the hand by turning it to the right as far as it will go.

2. Stand straight and keep your legs and hips still. Turn from the waist as far as possible to the back.

Rolling (Falling Rotation)

Any rotation where the part moving goes through a partial "fall" in space could be called rolling.

1. Turn your body over and over while lying on the floor.

2. Move the arms and hands continuously around each other.

3. Move your head in a very relaxed manner in a circle so that it "falls" as it goes forward.

4. Roll your hands at the wrists and your feet at the ankles.

Darting

Any movement that is quick and sudden, that shoots out or has a jabbing staccato quality, is called darting.

1. Do a jump just above the surface of the floor with both legs stretched wide and toes pointed. It is like a low split jump across the floor.

2. Any karate-type movement of the head, arms, elbows, legs, hips, or shoulders.

Jumping

To jump is to spring into the air from the ground, floor, or ice by using the muscles of the foot and leg to propel you. There are five basic ways you can jump.

1. From two feet landing on two feet.

2. From one foot landing on two feet.

3. From two feet landing on one foot.

4. From one foot landing on the same foot (hopping).

5. From one foot landing on the other foot.

Jumps can range from scarcely leaving the floor to jumps with a great deal of height and breadth.

1. Do running turns on your toes with small jumps.

2. Besides the single, double, and triple jumps in skating, your body can form various designs in the air as in split jumps, stag jumps, and mazurkas.

Bouncing

Bouncing in movement has the same feeling as a ball when it springs repeatedly from floor to air. This is a very interesting concept to apply to various parts of the body and results in the creation of unusual movements.

1. Bounce your body without the feet leaving the floor by using a knee action.

2. Bounce your hands, elbows, head, and other parts of your body in space.

Running

Running is moving rapidly through space with one foot lifting before the other one comes down. It can be done in all directions.

1. Run in a bouncy or springy manner, causing the torso to move up and down.

2. Run in a smooth, flowing way, with the torso remaining on one level.

3. Use just your hands and fingers to "run" through space.

Shaking

Shaking is a vibrating, trembling, or fluttering movement to and fro, up and down, or side to side of the whole or parts of the body.

1. Move your hands, performing a shaking design in space.

2. Shake your shoulders, head, and legs.

3. Wiggle your derriere.

Swinging

Moving to and fro or backward and forward rhythmically in a sweeping or swaying motion, as if suspended, can be called swinging. Swinging usually describes a curve in space.

1. Move your head in an arc from an up position to a down position and back up.

2. Swing each leg, arm, and hip in the same manner.

Pushing

Pushing is the act of pressing with force as if trying to move something away. Pushing can be done with every part of the body.

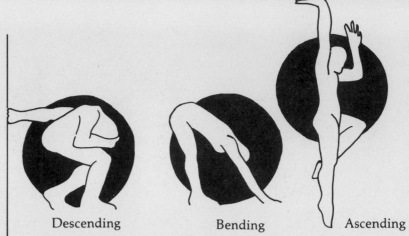

Fig. 15.
Elements of
movement.

Descending　　　　Bending　　　　Ascending

1. Flex the wrists and push with the palms away from the body into space.

2. Push your back away from your front, without moving the rest of your body, causing your torso to contract.

3. Push with your hip out to one side.

Pulling

Pulling is the opposite of pushing in that you are exerting a force to draw something toward you.

1. Reach both hands high above your head and pretend that you are grabbing a rope and pulling it down.

2. Push your shoulder out to the front and pull it back.

MOVEMENT EXERCISES

Read the directions for the following exercises carefully and use your imagination to carry them through. A thought to remember: at this point, you are not trying to make every movement look beautiful. You are only trying to solve the problem posed. If possible, get someone to do these exercises with you. It will be interesting to see the different approaches you will have to the same problem.

There is no such thing as a bad movement. Any movement can be valid in its proper place. It is wise to remind yourself

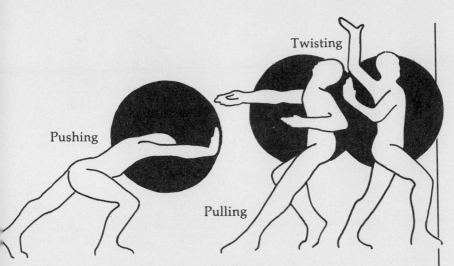

Pushing

Twisting

Pulling

that this is a learning process in an experimental atmosphere. There is no failure! Do not feel that every move you conceive must be of performance quality. At first they will be like artist's sketches that have to be filled in with texture and color before they are shown to critical eyes.

Movement Exercise 1. Go back over the list of elements of movement and compose a movement for each one. Think of using all the different parts of your body in the various compositions. Keep in mind that your motivation is the particular element with which you are working. Count out each movement as you compose it.

Movement Exercise 2. Perform the six movements pictured in Fig. 15. Do them one right after another without a break, to achieve an interesting movement phrase. You will have to insert slight transitions to blend the elements together.

Movement Exercise 3. Select three elements at random to work with. Using only these elements, compose two entirely different examples of each element. This will give you six different movements. Design your work to include the following:

a. Two movements will be done standing in one place.

b. Two movements will be done moving moderately about the floor.

c. Two movements will be done moving considerably about the floor, taking up a great part of the room.

To add color to your composition, include either a *forte* or *piano* dynamic, and a legato, marcato, or staccato articulation, making sure that every dynamic and articulation is used at least once. When you have finished composing the six movements, arrange them in such a way that the standing still movements are not necessarily together. The same would apply to the moderately moving and considerably moving pieces. There is no fixed rule for this, but you do want it to be varied and interesting. Some examples might be:

a. Standing still
    Moving considerably

    Moving considerably

    Moving moderately

    Standing still

    Moving moderately

b. Moving moderately
    Moving considerably

    Standing still

    Moving considerably

    Moving moderately

    Standing still

Before memorizing your movements, count them out and extend them to include whole, half, quarter, and eighth notes. You could write the music first and then create the movement if you like.

After memorizing the six movements in the order that you placed them, perform them together as one piece, making sure that there are smooth transitions between the moves. At this point, you may be dissatisfied with a particular move and wish to change it. Feel free to do so. After all, *you* are the choreographer and ultimately responsible for your own work. In the creative process, all rules can be broken. The important thing to remember is that it is the result that counts. You have a basis from which to work, so start those creative juices flowing!

Movement Exercise 4. Repeat Exercise 3, using various combinations from the following chart:

shaking	falling	bouncing	rolling
bending	pulling	falling	pushing
pushing	bending	jumping	bouncing
extending	descending	extending	descending
twisting	swinging	darting	ascending
turning	ascending	twisting	extending
bouncing	shaking	turning	darting
ascending	pushing	darting	turning
rolling	falling	pushing	jumping
shaking	ascending	shaking	pulling
darting	darting	jumping	twisting
rolling	rolling	rolling	jumping
descending	turning	swinging	twisting
swinging	twisting	descending	rolling
jumping	pulling	extending	shaking

bouncing	rolling	bending	descending
falling	pulling	turning	swinging
jumping	bending	jumping	ascending

Interesting movements to use in your skating programs can be composed by using different elements of movement by themselves or in combination with each other. Working out the elements on the floor will open you up to moving in a manner you may not have thought of before. The fun is in finding ways to transfer the movement from the floor to the ice. Some will be quite easy to transfer. Others may be more difficult, and that is when you will be challenged to make the changes necessary so that you can preserve the idea, or essence, of the movement you have composed. You can apply some of your new moves to jump landings or to positions coming out of spins.

I am not by any means eliminating the idea of using classical ballet movements. These, of course, are always beautiful and using them depends on your music. What we are trying to do is to find ways to invent or compose original movement to use in combination with the standard classical positions, which will make your program more interesting and somewhat special, a delight to watch. Learning the principles of movement, expanding and embroidering on them, will help you toward this goal.

Chapter 4

MOVEMENT FROM GESTURES

There is no abstract art. You must always start with something.
Afterward, you can remove all traces of reality.

—Pablo Picasso

Gestures can be used as a basis for finding fresh movement ideas. Gestures are behavioral patterns; things that you do physically with one or several parts of your body, like shaking hands in greeting, nodding your head "yes," and shrugging your shoulders for "I don't know." These movement symbols have been learned from infancy by exposure to cultural customs, through friendships and family environment. Some gestures are so obvious that they can be understood without words. For example:

1. Gently squeezing a loved one's hand.

2. Waving hello or goodbye.

3. Stamping your foot in anger.

Others are used reflexively or unconsciously:

1. Lowering your eyes when embarrassed.

2. Tilting your head to one side in uncertainty.

3. Pacing the floor in impatience.

MOTIVATION

Before a gesture is made, there is usually a thought that gives the reason for moving in a particular way. This is called motivation. Example: You have just skated in a national competition, and the judges have awarded you one 6.0 and the rest 5.9s. You joyfully give your coach a big hug. The gesture of hugging was motivated by the emotion of joy.

Motivation is the thinking process before a gesture is made.

There are two categories in which gestures can be placed:

1. Social

2. Emotional

Social Gesture

Many gestures describe the social communication that people have with each other during the course of a day. Some have positive intentions, while others have negative intentions.

Positive examples:

Handshakes	Embracing
Bows	Smiling
Waving	Beckoning
Kissing	Nodding

Negative examples:

Slapping/hitting	Shoving
Repelling with hand	Sticking tongue out

Stamping feet   Thumbing the nose

Frowning   Shaking a fist

Emotional Gesture

Each individual has a different way of expressing his or her emotions. Certain gestures are made consciously or unconsciously during pleasure or stress.

Examples of emotions:

Joy	Worry	Shame
Love	Excitement	Guilt
Sadness	Jealousy	Anger
Fear	Bravado	Uncertainty

Functional Activities

Functional activities are those that relate to the activities of the household and occupational hours.

Examples:

Combing hair	Shoveling
Brushing teeth	Carrying
Playing piano	Rowing a boat
Dusting furniture	Typing
Washing clothes	Throwing
Rocking babies	Pushing

ABSTRACTING GESTURES AND ACTIVITIES

When a gesture exactly represents what you are thinking or saying, it is called a literal gesture.

Examples:

1. Point to the moon and say, "Look at the moon."

2. Beckon to someone with your hand and pat a chair next to you, as if to say, "Come here and sit down."

3. Shake your head "No."

Literal gestures, which are common in drama, have almost no place in skating programs. (Literal gestures are sometimes effective in certain types of exhibition programs.) However, taking a literal gesture, extending it, then abstracting it, can change it into an artistic movement that can be used over and over again. Extending a gesture is expanding it and stretching it out in every way. It is the literal gesture, exaggerated.

To abstract a gesture or activity is to find a different way, perhaps using a different part of the body, to do the movement while maintaining the same motivating thought. This encourages you to use your limbs, head, and torso in ways you might not have thought of if you had not been trying to express a thought in abstraction.

Functional Activity Exercise 1. Go through the functional activity of brushing your hair. Move through the whole activity, recalling and doing everything in detailed pantomime, literally.

Literal steps to brushing the hair:

1. Walk to an imaginary dresser.

2. Look for the brush.

3. Pick it up.

4. Brush your hair.

5. Put it down.

6. Walk away.

Repeat this procedure several times until you are sure you have not omitted any detailed physical movement you make when actually brushing your hair.

Functional Activity Exercise 2. Go over the literal steps to brushing the hair, 1 through 6, this time extending each one.

Extended steps for brushing the hair:

1. Walk with large extended steps. Use the whole leg in an exaggerated manner. Swing your arms wide.

2. Move your head slowly as you "look for the brush." Touch imaginary articles, moving them around. The touching could be staccato in a *piano* articulation. (Refer to Chapter 2.)

3. Lift your arm high above your head and, with a large arc, bring it down to "pick up" the brush, raising it again to your head.

4. Go through the motions of brushing, lifting your arms high and using large extended brushing movements. Have the beginning of each stroke start high above your head and end as low as your arm can extend down, making outward circles.

5. Return the brush by reversing step 3.

6. Repeat step 1, reversing directions.

You are now ready to abstract the activity, and this is done by eliminating the literal completely, working only with the extended movements. Abstracting movements can become clearer to you if you relate it to abstract art. There are paintings and sculptures that are beautiful pieces of abstract art, whose titles seem to have little to do with the pieces themselves. The artist has a very definite intention of what is to be created and then proceeds to put into effect what he envisions with certain colors, form, and composition. It might be a fantasy of his thought. It doesn't matter if a painting entitled "A House in the Country" does not look like a typical country house. What matters is how the work affects you. Is it interesting in form? Do the colors haunt you with their beauty? Do you feel something when you look at it?

In skating, it is not important that your gestures be understood as far as your intentions are concerned. What does matter is that you make the audience feel something when you are expressing yourself.

To abstract is to get away from the realistic: It is an essence.

The way you abstract the extensions is a very personal creative act, unique to you. No two skaters using this same principle would produce abstract forms exactly alike. As you go through the extensions, experiment with several different ways to abstract each step until you find one that feels good to you. By working with the extensions, your abstractions will maintain the exaggerated quality that you need for performance. Your abstractions should go beyond that which is normal or natural.

Experiment with the following abstraction, using the steps in the extended gesture list as a dramatic guide.

Functional Activity Exercise 3. Abstracted steps for brushing the hair:

1. Walk backward, turning as you walk, swinging your arms in figure eight patterns.

2. As you "look for the brush," touch different imaginary articles with an elbow, shoulder, or wrist. Turn and reach your foot out waist-high in front. At the same time, start both arms moving from the back out to the front over the extended leg to "touch."

3. Extend both arms up as high as you can and curve them toward your right hip. Simultaneously, cross your right foot over your left. Pivot in a complete circle to the left, making small staccato stabbing movements with the hands in front of your torso for the "picking up brush" abstraction.

4. Use the whole body to "brush your hair" by lifting high on your toes and with control, contract your torso, curling over forward with your head close to your bent knees. Slowly release and extend your torso by starting an impulse action from the abdomen and stretching your body out slowly until you are standing straight. Repeat several times.

5. Reverse step 3 by pivoting first, making staccato movements; then turning and crossing feet. Bring curved arms from hip to high above head.

6. Walk and turn, using your elbows as focal points to perform "walking" movements in space.

Repeat these movements until you have established a form and can do all six steps without stopping. Put in transition movements if you need a connection. (Transition movements are those that connect one movement to the other.) You are now performing a small dance work that is an abstract piece and may not be identifiable with the literal activity that gave you the motivation to move in that particular way.

The time reserved each day for choreography and style allows you an excellent opportunity to transfer this small dance work to the ice. You will find more ways to abstract the movement now that you are using the skating medium. Use your dance abstraction as a base from which to work and try to transfer the essence and quality of what you have done to the ice.

Your walking could be cutbacks, crossovers, or footwork, using the abstract arm moves. The "picking up" of the brush might be a spread eagle, with the arm and head movements remaining the same as the dance piece. "Brushing the hair" could be a spin using the abstracted arms within the spin, or as you finish the spin.

Do not feel that you are tied to the movements you created on the floor. As you work you will find that what you have done may inspire you to work in a new direction. Experiment with whatever comes to your mind. You might create some fantastic move that will be named after you!

ADDITIONAL GESTURE AND ACTIVITY EXERCISES

Use the following ideas as exercises for abstracting gestures and activities. Follow the same format as for "brushing your hair." Do it literally first, expressing every detail. Imagine the physical structure you are in when performing the activity. How are you dressed? How are the people dressed around you? How does your head move; your eyes? What are the tensions in your body? Extend the gestures and activities, then abstract them.

1. You are being presented to royalty.

2. Throwing a basketball.

3. Greeting a loved one at an airport.

4. Peeling a banana.

EMOTIONAL EXPRESSION

Learning to abstract emotional gestures is an important step in becoming an expressive skater. If I could do one thing to influence the teaching of all beginning skaters, it would be to teach them to regard their bodies as live instruments that feel emotionally as well as physically. Then perhaps all skaters would develop the emotional motivation that is so essential to artistic skating. You probably have been told many times to smile during your program. This is certainly better than skating a whole program with a serious face, intent on accomplishing all the technical feats. But it is far better to express the emotions the music makes you feel through movements of the whole body. This can mean the difference between a good performance and a great performance.

Skating with feeling and expression comes naturally to some skaters. Others must work at it constantly through basic concepts, just as they do figures, jumps, and spins. The slow sections of your program can become a nonverbal communication with the audience by the use of expressive gestures stemming from a variety of emotions. You should be versatile and able to express yourself through any medium: jazz, ballet, modern dance, and dramatic.

Expressing emotions through body gestures will help form new artistic movements. Your emotions are unique to you, so you will express them differently from anyone else; but there are certain basic changes the body goes through when an emotion is shown that will help in determining expressive movement.

Emotion	Gesture
Excitement	Clasping yourself; jumping up and down; spinning around; explosive movements; clapping.
Sadness	Movements that are heavy, downward; movements toward the back; contractions; wavelike movements; rocking; drooping; distortions (see Fig. 16).
Joy/Happiness	Expansive movements; spinning around, successive movements; elevated movements (see Fig. 17).

Fear/Alarm   Raised shoulders; contractions; withdrawn body; repelling arms; fingers spread; limbs contracted; short spasms; leaning away; uncontrolled moves; palms flexed; hands passing over entire face (see Fig. 18).

Love   Hands touching the mid torso and upper cheeks; movements leaning forward; successive movements; round movements (see Fig. 19).

Bravado   Head turned away and raised; chest held high; upper torso straight; shoulders back; elbows away from body; swaggering, aggressive positions (see Fig. 20). Bravado is the affectation of bravery.

Imagine yourself in situations when you have experienced other emotions, such as worry, jealousy, uncertainty, anger, yearning, etc. When something pleasant or unpleasant happens to you, have one part of you stand aside and take notes. How do you feel? What does your body feel like? How does your body move? Your head? Your arms? Observe other people during emotional situations when words become inadequate and feelings are projected in physical movement. Add these other emotions to your list and describe how they make the body move.

When practicing the exercises, do not worry about whether they are working. Just focus on doing them and you will find they will work for you eventually as you relax into them. Get someone to do them with you. It will help to have constructive criticism while giving you the practice of showing emotions in front of someone. The more you practice the exercises, the easier it will get; and soon it will be nothing at all for you to show an emotional quality in front of an audience.

Emotion Exercise 1. Start with the first emotion of excitement, and find music that seems to fit it. Record a small section of the music on a cassette for practice purposes. Study the body

17.

provising happiness at the Ricky Harris Creative Workshop at
Olympic Ice Arena, Harbor City, Los Angeles, California.
m left to right: Allan Gonzales, Tracy Rowe, Sue Packard,
ky Harris. Photographer: Jerry Schwartz

16.

ter Lori Koshi portraying sadness. Photographer: Jerry
wartz

Fig. 18.
Depicting fear
and alarm
during Creative
Workshop at
the Ricky
Harris Dance
Studio. Skaters
from left
to right:
Patricia Neske,
Sue Packard,
Tracy Rowe,
Allan Gonzales.
Photographer:
Jerry Schwartz

Fig. 19.
Cyndi Lee
depicting love.
Photographer:
Paul Piazzese

Fig. 20.
Skaters Denise
Foster and
Patricia Neske
in a bravado
movement.
Photographer:
Jerry Schwartz

changes listed. Think of a situation, a little story, that involves excitement. It might be that you just won a French contest and the first prize is a trip to France. Envision how you would look when being told. How would you feel? How would you react? Improvise to the music using the gesture descriptions as a guide.

The face is a very important part of the expressive body. Let the emotion show on your face. Exaggerate everything. Raise your eyebrows; smile. Lose yourself in the music, concentrating on how the music helps you feel the emotion. Continue improvising until you find yourself repeating moves that feel good and look good. Remember them, jotting notes down if necessary. Spend as much time as you need to create movements that expressly indicate excitement. Try to feel the emotion inside as you move, and let your inner feelings guide you toward the exterior movement.

Emotion Exercise 2. Go over the movements you have just created and abstract any that are too literal. Do not reduce any of your facial expressions.

Emotion Exercise 3. Insert different dynamics and articulations (refer to Chapter 2) in your work.

Emotion Exercise 4. Check your elements of movement list, adding any that describe the emotion (refer to Chapter 3).

Emotion Exercise 5. Find music for the rest of your list of emotions and repeat exercises 1 through 4.

Emotion Exercise 6 (for two people). Use the following ideas for providing an emotional situation:

1. A confrontation between mother/daughter; son/father.

2. Two people; one jealous of the other.

3. Auditioning for a job.

Improvise movement following the emotional situation.

Practice the exercises until your muscles build a memory for the emotional reactions. Just when you think it will never happen, you will grasp the full meaning of your work, and that is when your development as an artist begins.

It is easy to be average. It is more difficult and takes more work to be daring, to try new things and create new forms. Think back to the careers of Toller Cranston and John Curry. These skating geniuses created new styles of moving on the ice. They traveled hard roads in their training years as they worked in ways different from most skaters. Cranston finished his amateur career as the 1976 Olympic Bronze Medalist. Curry was the Olympic Champion that same year. They both went on to great success in the professional world.

Fig. 21. Toller Cranston, 1976 Olympic Bronze Medalist. Photographer: David Leonardi

Some skaters are schooled to perform and move in ways that are almost flawless. These skaters are good athletes and fantastic technicians, but they may be average or mediocre artists, performing with little expression or feeling. On the other hand, many fine artists do not have an ounce of genius, but they work hard. The great artist is the one who does not depend entirely on inspiration or natural spontaneity the day of the performance.

Fig. 22.
John Curry, 1976 Olympic Champion. Photographer: William J.
Reilly

It is only through serious training in expression and movement that you become a great artist.

It is those who dare to be different that change the course of history. The avant garde, the forerunners of our time, are strong in their convictions about what they do. Be concerned only with *your* experimentation and practice. You know where you are going, and it is not the road of the average or mediocre skater. There is no such thing as complete perfection on your road, only the striving for it. You will look good after you have experimented with moves, working out their problems, the technique, and the artistry of execution.

Chapter 5

DESIGN IN SPACE AND TIME

*Space is not a static inert thing. Space is alive; space is imbued
with movement expressed by forces and counterforces; space vibrates
and resounds with color, light and form in the rhythm of life.*
—Hans Hoffman

Understanding movement design necessitates more concentration than in other visual arts. In painting you can
study the designs for as long as you want, comparing one
design with the other. In skating, movement designs are
not only made in space, but in the passage of time, and must
be remembered for comparison evaluation.

To explain the choreographic structure in movement, it
helps to compare it with the structure of written language, as
follows:

Language	Skating
Word	Body or tracing design in space and time
Phrase	Phrase pattern
Sentence	Phrase group
Paragraph	Section
Chapter	Fast or slow parts
Book	Complete program

Fig. 23.
The essence of
literal designs.

There are two
ways these
designs can
work in space:
(1) through
body designs
(2) through
tracing designs.

DESIGN IN SPACE

Every movement of your head and torso, as well as the way you place your arms and legs in space, causes changes in the shape of your body. Each change is a design in space. All designs are based on squares, circles, figure eights, curves, angles, and lines in every direction.

	Literal	Essence
Circle	○	⌣
Square	▭	⊓
Figure eight	8	⟨

Using geometric shapes as an inspiration for forming designs in space is another way to invent movement. You can use a shape literally, graphing it in the space around your body, or you can create a design that is the essence of the shape (see Fig. 23).

BODY DESIGNS

When you use the body and limbs to form a shape in space, it is called a body design. For example, when your body bends forward and forms a curve, it makes a visual shape that can be seen as long as your body is held in that position. Experiment with the following body designs:

Circles

1. Bend your right knee, raising the leg off the floor so that the thigh is parallel to the floor. (This actually forms a square design with that leg.) Bring the fingertips of both hands together under the raised leg, forming a circle with your arms.

2. With your knees slightly bent, feet together, arms above your head; curve your body over, allowing the arms to curve, until your fingertips touch your knees. You have formed a circle body design.

3. In a layback position, hold your skate, forming a circle.

See figure 24 for more ideas.

Janet Lynn: five-time U.S.
Ladies' Champion
(1969–1973); Bronze
Medalist, 1972 World
Figure Skating
Championships; Bronze
Medalist, 1972
Olympics.Photographer:
David Leonardi

Katarina Witt of (formerly) East Germany, 1984 and 1988 Women's Olympic Gold Medalist. Photographer: Ingrid Butt

Jill Trenary, 1990 Ladies' World Champion; 1987, 1989, and 1990 United States Ladies' Champion. Photographer: George Rossano

Denise Biellmann, Swiss Champion, 5th in Ladies' Division of the 1979 World Figure Skating Championships, Vienna. Photographer: Lyra Ward

Peggy Fleming: five-time U.S. Ladies' Champion (1964–1968); three-time World Champion (1966, 1967, 1968); 1968 Olympic Champion. Photographer: J. Keith Williams

Maia Usova and Alexander Zhulin of the USSR, 1989 World Silver Medalists in Dance, 1990 World Bronze Medalists in Dance. Photographer: George Rossano

Viktor Petrenko of the USSR, 1988 Men's Olympic Bronze Medalist, 1990 Men's World Champion. Photographer: George Rossano

Scott Hamilton, 1984
Men's Olympic Gold
Medalist; 1981, 1982,
1983, and 1984 Men's
World Champion.
Photographer: Charles
DeMore

Doug Williams and
Sharon Carz, 1990 World
Team Members, 1990
United States Pairs
Bronze Medalists, 1989
Pacific Coast Pairs
Champions, 1989 Pairs
Silver Medalists at World
University Games.
Photographer: George
Rossano

Marina Khimova and
Sergei Ponomarenko of
the USSR, 1989 and 1990
World Champions in
Dance, 1988 Olympic
Silver Medalists in Dance,
1984 Olympic Bronze
Medalists in Dance.
Photographer: Ingrid Butt

Christopher Dean and
Jane Torvill of Great
Britain, 1984 Olympic
Champions in Dance;
1981, 1982, 1983, and 1984
World Dance Champions.
Photographer: Ingrid Butt

The incomparable Belita—
first star of the Ice
Capades in 1940;
classically-trained ballet
dancer and partner of
Anton Dolin; musical
comedy, stage, and film
star. Photo courtesy Joe
Marshall. Photographer:
Constantine

Irina Moiseeva and
Andrei Minenkov, 1975
World Dance Champions,
ranked 2nd among 1978
Russian ice dancers, 3rd in
Ice Dancing at the 1979
World Figure Skating
Championships, Vienna.
Photographer: Lyra Ward

Ekaterina Gordeeva and
Sergei Grinkov, 1988
Olympic Champions in
Dance, 1987 and 1989
World Champions in
Dance. Photographer:
Ingrid Butt

Brian Boitano, 1988 Men's
Olympic Champion, 1986
and 1988 Men's World
Champion. Photographer:
Ingrid Butt

Tai Babilonia and Randy
Gardner, 1976, 1977, 1978,
and 1979 U.S. Pair
Champions; 1979 World
Pair Champions.
Photographer: David
Leonardi

With all my best wishes, and good luck Always Sonja Henie

Sonja Henie, ten-time
World Champion
(1927–1936), three-time
Olympic Gold Medalist
(1928, 1932, 1936).
Photographer unknown

Fig. 24.
Ricky Harris directing her Workshop's study of circle body designs. From left to right: Allan Gonzales, Ricky Harris, Tracy Rowe, Sue Packard, and Patricia Neske. Photographer: Jerry Schwartz

Squares

1. Start with your arms straight out to the side. Bend elbows so the fingertips point to the ceiling with your palms facing your body. This forms three sides of a square. Keeping the upper arm still, you can reverse the position, pointing the fingertips down. You could also have a position with one arm facing up, the other down.

2. Raise your leg parallel in the back with knee bent (parallel attitude). A turned-out attitude is also a square.

3. Raise your right arm straight up, pointing to the ceiling. The left arm forms a square when it is raised and bent at the elbow, with the fingers touching the inside of the right elbow.

4. The torso bent over in a ninety-degree angle, with the back leg high up in a parallel attitude, forms a square.

See figure 25 for more ideas.

Fig. 25.
Ricky Harris
watching
skaters in her
Creative
Workshop
forming square
body designs.
From left
to right:
Tracy Rowe,
Allan Gonzales,
Patricia Neske,
Sue Packard,
and Ricky
Harris.
Photographer:
Jerry Schwartz

Curves

1. Keep legs together and raise both arms straight above head. Bend the whole body over to one side in a curve.

2. One arm rounded in any direction makes a curve.

3. Bend back slightly to form a curve

Fig. 26.
Cyndi Lee
forming a
curved body
design.
Photographer:
Paul Piazzese

Figure Eights

1. Curve both arms and touch fingertips lightly to each side of the hip.

2. Do a layback and hold your free leg skate. Your other arm forms a circle with fingertips touching your chest.

3. One arm forms a circle, curving down at the side with fingertips touching your body, while your other arm curves up to form a circle by the fingertips touching your head.

Fig. 27.
Working on figure eight body designs. From left to right: Tracy Rowe, Patricia Neske, and Ricky Harris. Photographer: Paul Plazzese

Lines

1. One arm straight up, the other straight down at your sides.

2. Your body in a spiral position with a flat back; looks like a T.

3. Start with both arms out at the sides, shoulder level, palms flat. Bend one elbow with fingertips touching the inside of the shoulder; the other arm remains stretched to one side.

Fig. 28. Working on linear body designs in the Ricky Harris Dance Studio (from left to right): Allan Gonzales, Tracy Rowe, Sue Packard, Patricia Neske, and Ricky Harris. Photographer: Jerry Schwartz

TRACING DESIGNS

Tracing designs are those that are drawn in space with your limbs and other parts of your body. It would be the same as drawing a design in space with a signal flag (see Fig. 29). You cannot see the whole pattern at once, but you remember the design after it is made.

Fig. 29.
a. Tracing a figure eight design in space. b. Tracing a square design in space.

A good way to experiment with tracing designs is to practice body focus exercises, which call attention to shapes made by the way different parts of the body move.

Body Focus List

elbow	head
hip	arm(s)/hand(s)
shoulder(s)	knee(s)
foot	rib cage

Tracing Design Exercises

1. Draw your name in space with your hand, imagining large letters. Let your body move in any direction it needs to accomplish this. Repeat, using every body part listed above. You may have to jump to cross a t or dot an i.

2. Draw each geometric shape of circles, squares, figure eights, curves, and lines with different parts of your body.

3. Repeat the tracing designs in Exercise 2, adding different dynamics and articulations to each one (refer to Chapter 2).

PHRASE PATTERNS

A phrase pattern can be two or more designs in succession that are related to each other. For example:

Phrase Pattern 1. Stroke into an attitude body design. Follow with back crossovers, doing a tracing design with the arms. Continue with an inside three turn using a body or tracing design.

Phrase Pattern 2. Stroke into a series of change spirals, changing directions.

Phrase Pattern 3. Do an outside to inside spread eagle followed by an Ina Bauer.

PHRASE GROUP

A phrase group, like a sentence, makes an independent statement. It completes a purpose. Adding one or more phrase patterns to those listed above will make them into phrase groups.

Phrase Group 1. Add to Phrase Pattern 1 a back outside edge of the right skate. Step back on the left toe, quickly turning to step on the right toe going forward, and turning to jump into a flying camel combination spin with several changes of body design.

Phrase Group 2. Follow the change spirals in Phrase Pattern 2 with a stop, using a body or tracing design.

Phrase Group 3. Add to Phrase Pattern 3 two back dutch rolls to a double lutz.

SECTIONS

A section is made up of several phrase groups that are contained in the fast or slow parts of a program.

Slow and Fast Parts

A change of mood, not only in music, but also in movement, is required in a skating program. That is why there are slow and fast parts. It is more difficult and takes more artistry to skate with control and balance within slow, extended movements. Covering the ice in the slow parts is necessary, but not with the same intention as in the fast parts. Long extended stroking, with movements of the body performed slowly, can make the slow part a joy to behold. Occasional pauses here and there for expression can add immensely to the contrasting mood.

DESIGN IN TIME

There is a certain amount of time that passes as your program develops, with body and tracing designs forming phrase patterns, phrase patterns forming phrase groups, phrase groups forming sections. This establishes a design in time. Therefore, consider the overall shape of your movement sequences as to structure, content, and form. For a good design in time, one movement grows out of the other, and makes possible the next movement. There is also a relationship in time to the whole piece.

It is possible within a phrase pattern to have every body design in good form and with an interesting shape in space. But when fitting one design to another, the resulting design in time is unsatisfactory. The transitions may be poor, or perhaps do not go well with the music. Here is a case where the combination of good individual designs results in an unsatisfactory design in time. It is like fitting pieces of a mosaic together. Each

mosaic piece in itself may be beautiful, but it must also blend and fit with the pieces around it.

A design in time can take up a few moments of time or encompass a phrase pattern, a phrase group, a section, and so on, to the completion of the entire program. How you establish the design in time controls the artistry of the composition of the skating program. How you perform it is the artistry of the style.

Many skaters and coaches have a natural flair for designing movement in time; an innate sense of the flow of the phrase patterns following one another. Others can learn to choreograph more effectively by being more aware of shapes in space and their effect on each other through the process of time.

I highly recommend, if you are interested in choreography, that you spend some time whenever possible visiting art galleries and museums, looking at paintings and sculpture, as well as attending dance performances in every idiom. Many of the ideas that I have had for body design have come from these sources.

Practicing design exercises will eventually make designing for space and time a natural method of choreographing, and will result in a more interesting and vivacious program. If you understand this type of choreography, you will have a closer relationship to your skating, and feel a greater responsibility in carrying out your program.

Using Phrase Groups 1, 2, and 3, do the following:

1. Determine the time signature you want for each phrase group. Use four measures for each phrase pattern in the group. (Refer to Chapter 2.)

2. Select an emotion that will give you a motivation for each phrase group. (Refer to Chapter 4.)

3. Create body and tracing designs for the skating moves, using the elements of movement that will bring out the emotion. (Refer to Chapter 3.)

4. Add articulations and dynamics wherever suitable to add color and excitement to the designs. (Refer to Chapter 2.)

When you work on your program, try to consciously choreograph in time. Close your eyes and picture different body and tracing designs, connecting them together until a phrase pattern forms. Try them on the ice. Make changes. Practicing these choreographic techniques will help make your body a moving sculpture in space, an aesthetic experience. Through the use of design, dynamics, rhythm, and articulations, your program will become a work of art.

PART TWO

CREATING
A
SKATING
PROGRAM

Chapter 6

SELECTING & ARRANGING MUSIC

If I had my life to live over again, I would make it a rule to read some poetry and listen to some music at least once every week. The loss of these tastes is a loss of happiness.

—Charles Darwin

One of the important questions skaters ask each year is what music they should use for their new program. There is no one formula for this time-consuming, sometimes frustrating decision. Most skaters want something "different" in music. By different, they mean something that hasn't been used over and over again in skating programs. However, there are some skaters who prefer using music that has been used successfully by someone else.

WHO SELECTS THE MUSIC?

Many coaches select music for their skaters without the skater being involved in the selection. Other times, the selection is left entirely up to the skater. I believe the selection of music should be a cooperative effort between the coach and the skater. This of course would depend on the age and ability level of the skater involved.

MUSIC EDUCATION

Something that would be of great benefit to you would be a short course in music history, investigating the different composers, the periods in history in which they lived, their style of music, and how that style affects you. There are many good books in libraries and bookstores that can give you a background on the composers who lived in the baroque, classical, and romantic periods, as well as in our own time. Knowing the styles of these periods and the types of music that were written then can be very helpful when looking for music. You would be able to recognize a composer's name, connect it with a particular style of music, and know whether it might work for you.

A good idea is to keep a reference notebook just for music. Whenever you hear something you like, write down the name of the piece, the composer, and the conductor. When you find a particular affinity for one composer, there is a great possibility that you will like other music by him.

When you see a skating program that gives you good vibrations because of the way it works with the music, or parts of the program, write it down in your notebook. List the skater, the skater's level, and as much as you can find out about the music. If you ask enough questions, someone will know what the music is. There may be a time later on when you will want to use part of that music, or another piece by the same composer. Getting that skater's music, listening to it, and analyzing its construction and how it worked with that particular program can be an aid to you in your future choreographic process.

Skating demands a certain excitement in the music. That does not mean that you cannot do a perfectly marvelous program to music that does not have *crash! zip! bang! boom!* in it all the time. It depends on what your body is like and what kind of a skater you are.

One of the most beautiful programs I have seen was the exhibition program skated by Charles Tickner, the 1978 U.S. and World Men's Champion, to the Moonlight Sonata, by Beethoven, choreographed by his coach, Norma Sahlin. The predominant point in his whole program was the way he felt his music. He skated with a reverence for every move that he made, and this was connected to what he was hearing in the music. This feeling showed from the very beginning as he stood waiting for his music to begin. As I watched the expression on his face and in his body, I knew I was going to see something special. It was as if the music had already started within him, and when we heard the first note, it was an extension of what he was already hearing. It was poetry in motion; one of the most beautiful experiences I have had in skating. What Charles felt was so strong that it made every member of the audience feel the music too.

Fig. 30.
Charles Tickner, 1978 and 1979 U.S. and 1978 World Men's Champion, skating to the Moonlight Sonata. Photographer: David Leonardi

When you are considering music for your new program, it should be music that makes you feel something. It doesn't matter if some other skater has used it in the past, or if you find, after selecting it, that a current skater is using it. What is important is the way *you* relate to the music. What you personally feel about it will cause you to skate it in a way that will be different from anyone else.

Your coach and parents can help analyze how mature you will be in one year, not only physically, but emotionally, and try to evaluate what your skating abilities will be by the time this music and your routine must be performed. This should be a very important part of your music decision.

The emotional quality in the music is important to consider for the artistic feeling of your program, but you also have to consider what type of music can help you best carry out the necessary skating elements. What kind of music will help you carry out your footwork? Your jumps? Your spins?

SOURCES OF MUSIC

Listen to music whenever you can. Don't wait until you need new music. There are good classical and contemporary radio stations that you can turn on during your trips to and from the rink that will help develop your musical tastes. As you listen, analyze the music for its dynamics and articulations. Try to identify the legato, marcato, and staccato sections, as well as when the music is *forte* and *piano.* (See Chapter 2.) This will assist you in recognizing music that will work for skating. When you hear something you like, purchase it right away, or jot the name and description of the music in your notebook to refer to later when you need new music.

There are other economical ways to find music. One is access to your coach's music library. Almost every coach who has been teaching for any length of time has collected a vast number of records and tapes. You don't want to invade the privacy of a pro's leisure hours, which are few, but you might be able to persuade him or her to bring some music to the rink when you could have a music listening session.

There was a time years ago when you could go into a record shop and listen to the records you were thinking of buying. This was very simple and economical compared to the procedures today. Coaches and skaters spend a great deal of time and money buying music with the hope that they will find something they can use. Although some of this music may be good, it may not be suitable for a skating program. Some record stores have available records that they play in the store during the day, and if it happens to be something you want to hear, you are in luck.

Go to a small record store with personalized service. There is a small classical music store that I use because the owner seems to know every piece of music in his stock. He has such a love for all music that you get excited just being there with him. Sometimes I will come in knowing that I will be using a particular piece of music for a section and ask him to suggest something to go with it for another section. Because he knows the music so well, he many times is able to find just the right combination. He can also suggest recordings of the same music that have better orchestrations. Setting up a personal relationship with someone like this can be of great value to you.

Investigate the many available albums of ballet music. Because it is danceable, there is a good chance that ballet music will make good skating music. Overtures to operas should also be considered. I once found an excellent album of overtures to operas. The music was very suitable for skating and the dynamics were excellent.

Another place to look for music is in the library. Many libraries have extensive record collections and you can check out records to listen to at home. Even if they do not have the latest recordings, you will find many classical as well as musical comedy albums that could be of service to you.

Colleges and universities with music departments usually have listening labs where students can go and listen to music as long as they want, in soundproof rooms. Some of these schools also have listening rooms in their libraries where you can use a card index file to find music by composer or title. The music is usually recorded on tapes. Libraries that have this type of service carry a large stock of all kinds of music.

The Schwann catalogue is a periodical that can be purchased at most music stores and is also available for use in libraries. The catalogue has all the classical composers listed in alphabetical order, and the years in which they lived. This gives you some idea of time periods. As music reflects the time period, you will be able to detect the kind of music written by a composer. For example, skating to a Mozart piece, in my opinion, needs a style that works strictly with that time period. On the other hand, I feel Bach is more universal, and inspires exploration into more contemporary avenues.

Using the Schwann catalogue, you can also tell what country the music comes from. A lot of Russian music reflects the nation, and works very well in skating programs. On the other hand, Stravinsky, a more recent Russian composer, wrote music that was more international which inspires more contemporary ways of moving. Once you know periods and composers, you can somewhat get an idea of the sound. The Schwann catalogue is a reminder. If you want to be very contemporary, look at the list of composers who are still living and are comparatively young. The catalogue lists contemporary as well as classical music, with album numbers.

If you are going to use jazz, disco, or other contemporary music forms, one thing to consider is the sameness in dynamics. When you use music that has the same qualities, tempo, and accents in every measure, you end up skating to a background of music, rather than being able to interpret the music. This does not always apply to exhibition programs where you can get very theatrical and flamboyant. Good rock, disco, and jazz that have the necessary qualifications for interesting movement and interpretation can be effectively used for competitive programs.

The forms of electronic music and music concrete are being used extensively in the dance world. Electronic music is music produced by electrical equipment. Music concrete is made up of sounds of actual things which are then sometimes distorted. This kind of music can be interpreted very well and the cutting of the music is very easy. Interesting effects can be obtained with music concrete. It may not work for a whole piece, but for a dramatic and dynamic effect, a small part of this music could be very exciting, as long as it works with the pieces around it.

At one time it was thought that voices could never be used in skating programs. (Voices have been used in skating programs without words, as well as parts with humming.) This type of music is very effective in exhibition programs. When you use voices for an exhibition program, listen to the words and make sure you are skating to something you want to skate to, as far as the lyrics are concerned. Also consider the type of voice that is singing, and whether your age and personality can relate to it.

Before you make up your mind definitely about a piece of music, take it out on the ice and improvise to it. That is the best way to tell if you are going to be able to skate to it. If you can get some sort of an emotional quality from the inside to form skating moves, then you know you have the right music.

If you are considering some kind of nationalistic music, make sure that you will be able to educate yourself in some of the moves representative of that country. It is important that you carry out the feeling of the music in the movements.

When you listen to music, listen with the idea of interpretation and skating element values. Are there places for spins and design movements? Listen in a different way than you would when you are listening just for pleasure. Remember you only have from two to five minutes and you must get everything across during that time. It must have all the elements of variety and contrast, as well as content and form. That is why music has to be cut, as you don't always find all the necessary elements you need in a short section of one piece. Some of the best skating programs are those that use different sections from the same ballet, symphony, or concerto. There is a higher degree of satisfaction and musicality to the program when it is done in this manner.

ARRANGING MUSIC

You should have a plan as to how many parts you want in your program. The following gives three examples:

1. Slow-fast-slow-fast

2. Fast-slow-fast

3. Fast-slow-fast-slow-fast

Some skaters and coaches make the arrangement decision before they look for music, and research accordingly. Others make this decision during the musical selection process. Programs of shorter duration usually follow the format of fast-slow-fast, as it simplifies the time factor, and enables the music to flow without being in danger of sounding too chopped up.

In four- or five-minute programs, you can easily do whatever you prefer. The programs that start with a slow part can be an advantage to the skater, as it actually shortens the program as far as stamina is concerned. You are not pushing hard until you are already into the program, and you are able to concentrate on the emotional quality without feeling the pressure of being tired.

On the other hand, there is something wonderful about a beautiful, long slow part which you can do within the format of fast-slow-fast. The time allows you to carry through a quality based on a motivating thought or story, and enables you to captivate the audience with its magic. Your decision should be made not only in accordance with your existing stamina, but what you expect it to be by the time you must perform in your major competition after a year of training.

Another point to consider is the blending of the music between the fast and slow parts. Many skating records are put together very hastily with sad results. Some of these programs have a fast part going into a slow, or vice versa, with no transition. There should always be consideration given to the blending of the last note of one part and the first note of the following part. Even though you might end one part with a stop, consider trying to begin the next part either with the same note, an octave higher or lower, or one that is within the harmonic interval of a related chord, that would give the feeling of a transition. I have known very musical skaters, who have a lot to do with selecting their own music, look for just one note out of an entirely different piece, to tape into their music to give that kind of transition. If the music in the last part of your program has a dull ending, but you like everything else about it, it is perfectly all right to find an ending from an entirely different piece of music. This might mean cutting in a phrase of two or four bars, several notes, or perhaps only one note.

Spending a lot of time in finding your ending first will make finding a beginning much easier. You want your music to end on a "high," making everyone wish they could hear and see more, yet you do not want the music to take over and belittle your skating. As I said before, your choice depends a great deal on your abilities. If you are a very strong skater, then you can take very strong music. If your skating needs strengthening, too strong music will make it look weaker. Know your ability, know your music, and plan accordingly. The selection and arrangement of your music can be very gratifying when you get the proper results. Start early enough in the year so you will have plenty of time to research the music that will make yours a very special program.

Now that you have selected and arranged your music, and have a record or tape, the next step is getting to know it well. The best way to do this is to play your music over and over until it almost becomes a part of you, and you are able to hum the whole composition. Knowing your music this well is a great aid when designing ice patterns for your new program.

Chapter 7
ICE PATTERNS

When schemes are laid in advance, it is surprising how often the circumstances fit in with them.

—Sir William Osler

The composition of a skating program is based on the structure of an ice pattern. As you move across the ice, the eyes of the viewers draw a design. If you go around several times in a circle, the eye will follow that design and it will seem monotonous. When designing your ice patterns, it is important that you use a variety of areas for jumps, spins, and other spectacular effects. The whole ice area should be utilized to make the program interesting. Many coaches and skaters do this with a natural feeling for ice design, but sometimes find themselves repeating the same patterns in other programs. Having a method for designing ice patterns will help to eliminate this problem.

WAYS TO DESIGN ICE PATTERNS
There are two ways to proceed in designing ice patterns:

1. Lay out your program on the ice; then draw it on a sheet of paper to see if it has balance, symmetry, and asymmetry for stimulation and excitement. Make changes in the program to correct any problems in design.

2. Design your program on paper first, then choreograph to fit the design.

The advantage of the latter is that much of the work designing your program can be done off the ice with the additional benefit of having your music available to play as much as you like. This way, you can learn every nuance in the music, the dynamics and articulations, and where all the dramatic effects are to be used for jumps, spins, and footwork. Seeing a drawing of your ice moves will keep you from repeating one pattern too many times and guide you into designing a more artistic program.

DESIGNING ICE PATTERNS OFF THE ICE

The following procedure can be a guide in designing your program off the ice.

Listen to your music carefully and repeatedly until you determine which jumps and spins will fit into the different parts, and where your footwork will be. During this time you will also find musical places for any special skating effects you wish to include in your program. With a stopwatch, go over the music and record the time it will take for each element listed, and the time that elapses from the end of one element to the beginning of the next one. This gives you an idea as to how long you will have for patterns between your elements.

Number and list the elements in appropriate columns on a chart, leaving enough space between each item for recording the passage of time. The chart shown on page 74 is an example of a senior lady's four-minute program. The same kind of chart can be used for pairs and dance.

Draw two ovals for each part of your program on a sheet of paper. The ovals represent the ice surface. Check the elements you want to accomplish and think of floor patterns that would facilitate that result. Perhaps you could think of a different floor pattern with a surprise to accomplish the same element, instead of following the same pattern that you have used before. An element of surprise in a program is always welcomed by judges and audience, such as an unconventional place for beginning or ending your program.

Work with three or four elements at a time, placing them in the ovals by number. Keep in mind the time factor so you

Fast	Slow	Fast
(1 min. 6 sec)	(2 min. 1 sec)	(53 sec)
1. Beginning Pose	7. Stop	14 Camel Spin
7 seconds	23 seconds	2 seconds
2. Tuck Axel(3 sec)	8. Double Loop(4 sec)	15. Footwork(10 sec)
10 seconds	7 seconds	to an
3. Triple Salchow(4 sec)	9. Layback(8 sec)	16. Open Axel(3 sec)
21 seconds	21 seconds	11 seconds
4. Double Axel(3 sec)	10. Double Flip(4 sec)	17. 3 Russian Splits(10 sec)
4 seconds	30 seconds	1 second
5. Double Axel(3 sec)	11. Double Axel(3 sec)	18. Arabian(3 sec)
2 seconds	8 seconds	to
6. Flying Layover(7 sec) Camel	12. Spread Eagle(2 sec)	19. Flying Camel(6 sec) to Sit Spin
1 second	to a	1 second
7. Stop(1 sec)	13. Double Lutz(3 sec)	20. Blur Spin(5 sec)
	2 seconds	21. Stop(1 sec)
	14. Camel Spin(6 sec)	

know approximately how much ice you have time to cover before the next element must be performed. Begin drawing a pattern going from one number to the next, using the geometric designs of squares, circles, lines, curves, and figure eights as a basis. Try to form patterns in a variety of ways. Instead of crossovers in a circular pattern for the entrance to a spin, try a straight line pattern on a diagonal, or across the width of the rink. You might even use the design of a square with some change spirals causing a sharp-cornered square to occur. Follow this with a straight line pattern of chainé turns into the spin.

Long curved ice patterns are conducive to beautiful edges and should be used in your program. If you are not an "edge" skater, learn to be one; for that is what gives skating its flow.

Designing curves in your program and choreographing long edges to fit will help develop you into an edge skater.

As you think of ideas for moves on the patterns, jot them down in the time spaces provided between elements on the chart. The use of colored pencils for the different paths between elements on your oval will help make the design clearer. At this point you may want to change one of the patterns if it does not suit you. Keep experimenting until you are satisfied that the pattern pleases you and will fit your skating capabilities.

When you finish your first part, look at the designs and see if you have covered the ice and have a feeling of flow. Continue until you have designed the entire program, using five or six ovals. Look at each oval and compare them with each other to see if you have used a variety of patterns. Also check to see if your ice patterns are balanced and you have located your spins and jumps in contrasting areas.

You will probably make some changes when you try the program on the ice, but you will have a good foundation from which to work, and have confidence that you have an artistic ice pattern.

Figures 31, 32, 33, 34, and 35 are examples of one way to design the four-minute program as listed in the time chart.

Whether you are a beginning, intermediate, or advanced skater, planning your ice patterns will help make your program more effective. In the next chapter, you will learn how to create the movements that will fit your ice patterns and connect one element to the other.

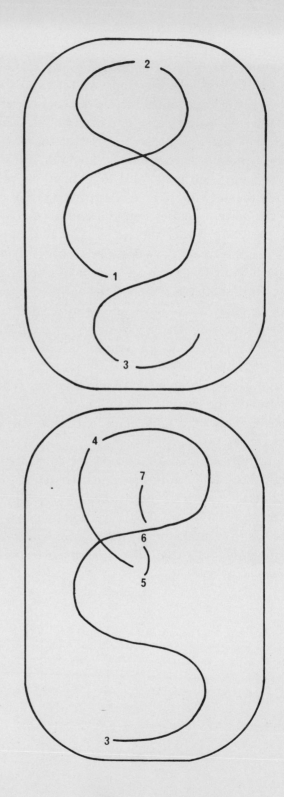

Fig. 31.
Ice pattern for beginning of first fast part of four-minute program following time chart.

Fig. 32.
Ice pattern for end of first fast part of four-minute program following time chart.

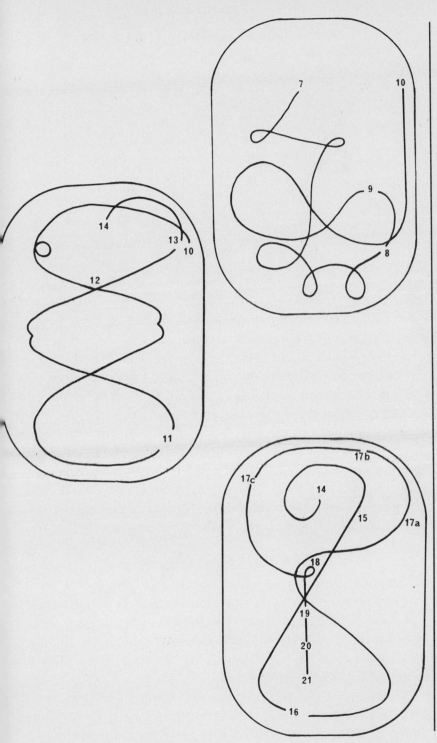

Fig. 33.
Ice pattern for beginning of slow part of four-minute program following time chart.

Fig. 34.
Ice pattern for end of slow part of four-minute program following time chart.

Fig. 35.
Ice pattern for last fast part of four-minute program following time chart.

Chapter 8

CHOREO-GRAPHING MOVEMENT

Intention causes the effort which creates the shape.

—Eugene Loring

One of the responsibilities in choreographing movement for composition and style is to incorporate the technical and artistic elements in such a way that when the program is over, it can be remembered for its emotional quality as well as its design. Skating, being a sport and an art, must satisfy the requirements of the sport and the aesthetic qualities of the art. This is a difficult undertaking if it is not done skillfully. Try to include artistic ingredients that complement the technical elements that are to be performed in order to receive points. Developing a motivating force will make these elements into an exciting spectacle in the fast parts and an emotional experience in the slow parts.

LINKING MOVEMENTS

In Chapter 7 you learned how to make an outline of your program, listing the various elements that fit into specific places in the music. In most fast parts, where there are short amounts of time between the elements, there are linking movements that are transitions going away from or toward spins, jumps, and footwork.

When the time factors between the elements in slow parts are wider apart, there is more freedom to focus on an interpretive presentation, rather than just reaching a specific point.

Here is an opportunity to create movements for style and emotional quality.

CONTINUITY OF EMOTION

Motivation should come first in deciding what gestures can be used with the skating transitions to reach your skating goals and interpret your music. The gestures are then extended and abstracted into movements that are strong enough to have an emotional impact on the audience. You need to establish and sustain a continuity of emotion throughout the entire performance.

Audiences at exhibitions and shows will remember less of the technique and separate steps of a program and more of the continuity of emotion. Skaters find it difficult to sustain this in their competitive programs as their thoughts are involved with accomplishing the necessary elements. No one can teach you how to feel, but you can learn vivid forms of expression that can be used in your connecting moves, which will help support a continuity of emotion. These forms of expression can vary according to your temperament and what you wish to express.

MOTIVATION

One way to develop a continuity of expression is to create movement that follows a dramatic outline inspired by your music. This is like a libretto of an opera, a script of a play, or a short story that has a beginning, a middle, and an end. You may think of just one line of a play or a poem that the music brings to mind; or you may think of one word that you could create a story around.

Listen to your music over and over and fantasize until an idea comes to you. Let your thoughts wander as you listen, until one idea begins to form. Do this for several days and every time you listen to your music, continue developing your idea. Know who you are or who you want to be while skating your program. Who are you relating to in your story? Is it a real or imaginary character? When you find that you are thinking of the same story every time you listen to your music, begin writing it down. Be sure to leave plenty of room between each line of your story for descriptive notes. Check your time chart and ice patterns to be sure that your notes coincide with each time factor and pattern.

DESCRIPTIVE NOTES

Begin your descriptive notes by determining the emotions involved in your story. Read one sentence of your story at a time and write the emotion that fits underneath a word or a phrase. As your story progresses and changes, so will the emotions. When you have finished, put your music on and read the emotions to the music. Do all the emotions relate well to the music? Make changes in your story and emotions whenever and wherever you feel it is necessary.

The articulations and dynamics of your story should be noted next. If you have written "happy" as your first emotion, decide whether this is *forte* happiness because it is so exuberant, or if it is *piano* for quiet happiness. Noting whether it is *forte* or *piano* will help you to determine whether the move for that place in your program will be one with a lot of tension behind it, or one with less effort involved. The music will help you determine these dynamics, as well as whether you should have legato, staccato, or marcato as your articulations. (Refer to Chapter 2.) Record the articulations next to the dynamics and emotions.

At this point, check your list of elements of movement (Chapter 3) and add the ones that apply to your story and descriptive notes. With "happiness, *piano,* legato," you may want to write "bending, extending, turning." With "frustration, *forte,* staccato," you may want to add "darting, twisting, kicking." Record whether you feel the move should be in a circular, square, curved, figure eight, or linear design. Check your descriptive notes with your story and music several times until you are satisfied you have an interesting and varied one.

EXAMPLE OF STORY (Relates to time chart and ice patterns in Chapter 7)

Fast Part

1. **Beginning pose**
   The people in the palace courtyard
   7   anticipation

   s   *piano*
   e
   c   legato
   o
   n   swinging
   d   running
   s   rolling

       curves

2. **Tuck Axel—3 seconds**
   became tense
   10   worried

   s   *piano*
   e
   c   staccato
   o
   n   darting
   d   bouncing
   s   shaking

       lines

3. **Triple Salchow—4 seconds**
   as the two groups   *of dissenting factors*
   21   frustration   anger

   s   *piano*   *forte*
   e
   c   marcato   marcato
   o
   n   extending   pulling

d   turning
s   ascending

square

pushing
twisting

figure eight and
lines

4.   Double Axel—3 seconds
met
4   bravado

s   *forte*
e
c   marcato
o
n   ascending
d   twisting
s   pushing

squares

5.   Double Axel—3 seconds
for a confrontation
2   determined

s   *forte*
e
c   staccato
o
n   extending
d
s   line

6.   Layover Flying Camel—7 seconds
under the blazing sun.
1   excited

s   *forte*
e

c   marcato

o

n   extending

d

s   line

7. Stop—1 second

Slow Part

Suddenly, a hush fell over the crowd as the

23   anticipation

s   *piano*

e

c   staccato

o

n   bending

d   turning

s   darting

    lines and curves

8. Double Loop—4 seconds
old priest appeared
7   reverence

s   *piano*

e

c   legato

o

n   twisting

d   bending

s   shaking

    curves

9. Layback—8 seconds
with the beautiful young queen.

21 loving

s *piano*
e
c legato
o
n bending
d extending
s ascending
   turning

   circles and curves

As an exercise, finish writing the story to fit the time chart in Chapter 7. Fill in descriptive notes for the balance of the slow part and the ending fast part.

CREATING THE MOVES

With your story and descriptive notes completed, you now have a firm basis for creating the moves that will fit between the elements in your program. Check your time chart and ice pattern for the first move you need to choreograph. Play your music to see how much of the story you will be using. Mark off that section in your story with the number 1. (See example of story.) Continue doing this until your complete story is divided into the numbered sections that match your time chart and ice patterns.

Using an off-ice area for creating your moves is a big time-saver. You can do it at home or in the ballet room of your rink, if there is one. This will allow you more time for experimentation, as well as being able to play your music as much as you like.

As you begin to choreograph, keep checking your descriptive notes. Use the literal ideas and abstract them into skating movement. Allow your body to respond to any thought that comes to your mind. It doesn't matter if you do a move that you think is funny or awkward. It may lead to another move that is exactly the right one.

When you have your moves for your first section, write

them down so you will not forget them, and go on to the next section. Continue in this manner until you have completed the first part of the program. Now is the time to transfer your choreography to the ice, making the body moves work with skating moves. Try to keep as many of your ideas as possible while you incorporate your moves with three turns, mohawks, crossovers, pivots, etc. You will probably be surprised at the new artistic moves you have created when you transfer them to the ice.

There may be some moves that do not work on the ice, but try to use the essence of the move in some way. Go through all the parts of your program using this format until you have finished.

ARTISTIC SUGGESTIONS

1. Gestures of the head will enhance the moves you create. The whole feeling of what you are trying to portray will become clearer when you allow your head to be involved.

2. Use all the directions in which your head can move:
   a. Downward
   b. Upward
   c. Tilting
   d. Side to side
   e. Rolling

3. Use your head with control, as well as tossing it backward or forward for dynamic accents. Try to always follow an action of a hand with your eyes. This will give your head a more expressive quality.

4. The face is an important expressive area and reflects what you are thinking; so be sure to think about what you want to express.

5. Consider the contrast between even and uneven shapes. No matter how well it is performed, if the entire program incorporates only symmetrical designs, it will be dull. Oppositions are strong and forceful. Parallel movements are serene and decorative.

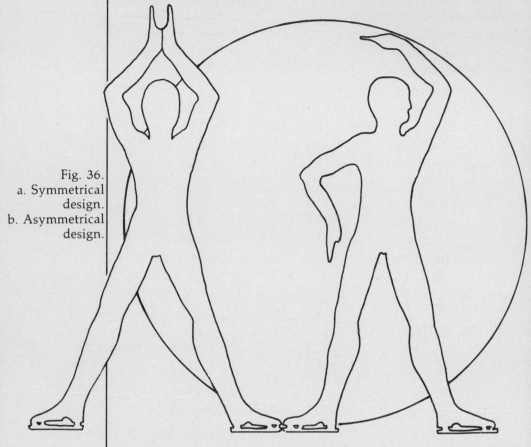

Fig. 36.
a. Symmetrical design.
b. Asymmetrical design.

6. Gestures of the hands have different implications and can be meaningful in carrying out your ideas.
    a. Palms down
    b. Palms up
    c. Palms forward
    d. Palms vertical
    e. Palms clutching
    f. Making a fist

7. Experiment with gestures in which the hands touch the

face, head, shoulders, waist, knees, hips, and feet, when working on spins as well as linking moves.

8. Using a body focal point for tracing designs will add variety to your choreographic moves. Trace a design with your:
    a. Shoulder
    b. Elbow
    c. Wrist
    d. Hand
    e. Chest
    f. Waist
    g. Hip
    h. Thigh
    i. Knee
    j. Ankle
    k. Derriere
    l. Foot (The foot touching the ice in different ways will give you ideas for footwork.)

9. Choreograph your program so that there is a constant building toward an exciting end. Save some of your best moves for the last part of your program, as this will leave the strongest impression on your audience.

10. Value the communication of simplicity. Many times, the sections that contain the most simple concepts are ultimately the most successful ones.

Above all, do not get discouraged. Miracles do not happen overnight. Practice the three Ds:
                discipline
                dedication
                determination

Go over each chapter in the book thoroughly until you understand the theories they contain. Be humble; ask for help if you need it. One little word from someone may cause that light to switch on! Hard work and complete commitment to your performance goals will change what seemed like ordinary movement into a work of art. The different degrees in which dynamics, articulations, energy, rhythm, design, and motivations are used, can result in a thrilling and memorable program.

Chapter 9

POLISH
AND
PERFORM

Diamonds are chunks of coal that stuck to their job.
—Forbes Epigrams

N ow that your program is choreographed, the real work begins. All the ingredients are there and you will practice, hone, and polish, paying attention to the most minute details, in order to get your program ready for critical eyes. Discipline, dedication, and a wholehearted commitment will transform your program into a work of art.

Make a distinction between times when you are training the body and times when you are rehearsing for a performance. First you train and prepare, then you rehearse. If you rehearse all the time, you run the risk of developing bad habits which are difficult to break. I have observed skaters going through their programs repeatedly, making errors in movement sequences, yet never taking the errors out of the program by spending time to train their bodies to execute these maneuvers properly. Instead, they keep repeating the program, hoping that the next time it will be right. This is the long way toward the achievement of a good performance.

SPOT PRACTICE

Frequent run-throughs are necessary as they give a feeling of continuity and fluidity. Going through your program twice during each skating session will strengthen the whole structure of your work, as well as develop stamina. If it is difficult to get

your music played the second time, skate your program without it. By this time you know your music so well, you will be able to hear it in your head.

Spot practices, however, can also be an important part of your daily schedule. This is when you can focus your attention on the details of timing, characterization, and artistic moves, as well as jumps and spins. One way to spot practice is to take a small section out of the middle of your program. The reason for starting in the middle is that there are movements on either side that can be worked on, then added as they are polished. If you get the middle secure, you can then work on the transitions toward the beginning and toward the end. Making the middle of your program strong right away gives you someplace that you are going to and away from, until you are able to build up the rest of the program.

You may start with just eight or sixteen counts. Let us call this small piece section A. Practice section A over and over until you fully understand every detail. What emotion should you be feeling? Concentrate on extending every movement. Do your transitions blend with the elements in that section? Respond to every detail until you reach a full understanding of the movements.

At times you may have to practice in slow motion, even though the finished movement will be done quickly, precisely, and with lightning clarity. After you master the choreographic pattern, you can gradually increase speed until it is skated at the correct tempo. Then practice it to the music. A small portable cassette recorder that you can place on the rail is handy for this type of spot practice, so that you can use the music as much as you like. It may take days, even weeks, until section A is polished and you are performing it well. Don't get discouraged. Keep working at it as long as it takes to polish it into jewellike perfection. At the same time, you will be doing complete run-throughs of your program at each session.

When section A is polished, take another small piece that comes just before it. Call this section B. Work on section B in the same manner. When section B is polished, combine it with section A and practice both together as one section. Section C will be a piece on the other side of section A. (See Fig. 37.) You will keep working in this way, toward the beginning and end of your program.

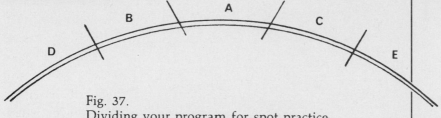

Fig. 37.
Dividing your program for spot practice.

BUILDING MUSCLE MEMORY

Working on repetitive patterns is absolutely necessary for mastering the movements in your skating program, and building a memory for them in your muscles. Drill, though, does not need to produce a dry or stale program. If you plan so that you are developing a new quality each time, you will look forward to your practices, and your program will stay alive.

Do not hesitate to put time into the smallest details of your program. It is this giving of your time that reaps the rewards. In practice you cannot expect to execute your movements and maneuvers perfectly right away. You will achieve quality by working on fine details. Even though you may perform at an early age, it still takes many years before you have the physical and emotional maturity to be an artistic skater with excellence. You cannot rush that. But if you really love what you are doing, you can do it every day, and work hard, and it does not matter, because you are loving what you are doing.

Nothing can be achieved without bodily struggle. You will go through many periods when you are falling, perhaps even looking clumsy and making errors. It is useless to kick the ice, act sullen, scold yourself, or take out your frustration through other negative energies. You cannot gain the quality of perfection in performance until you go through making mistakes when you practice. When skaters behave in this way it is from the fear that they will not be able to perform their work, and this fear comes out in anger. Detailed practices will decrease your fear and give you confidence. If you recognize the human capacity to make mistakes, you will have a different attitude

and be able to turn your negative energies into positive energies through self-evaluation and an analysis of what you are doing.

When something goes wrong in your practice—when you have not correctly performed a step, a sequence, a spin, or a jump—look at it in this way: if you have done it once correctly, then you know that you are aware of all the ingredients that make it work. Therefore, if it does not work, it means that you have left at least one of those ingredients out. Instead of getting angry and upset with yourself, stop and go over all the ingredients that need to be applied to make that jump, spin, or movement sequence work correctly. If you look at it logically, you will find that you have forgotten to do something. It may be the check of a shoulder, or the placement of one arm. There is just so much of this you must go through before things begin to evolve and fall into their proper places.

There is a story about Picasso that relates how, as a young artist, he spent a whole year sketching bulls. He drew many bad ones, but kept drawing them until one day he looked at a bull he had sketched, felt satisfied with it, and thought it was a good bull. After that he did not have to think when he painted a bull. It just flowed from his fingers, for the memory in his muscles was there. You will be developing muscle memory through repetition and this leads to good performances. Your mind is then freed to concentrate on the emotional qualities and the performance of the program.

Some skaters do their exercises diligently and precisely, but without a flicker of love or even excitement for what their bodies are executing. Nothing seems to be connected with the exultation of skating. Even when they are introduced to the most glorious movement, they remain unaffected, which makes them perform movements as if they were merely doing a job.

Artists will work on something hundreds of times until it becomes natural, and while they are working, they are enjoying the exhilaration of the movement itself and loving what they are doing.

CONCENTRATION AND FOCUS

You cannot have concentration without discipline. To do a jump well, you must check; so you discipline your body to check. You discipline yourself to concentrate for many minutes at a time on the same school figure. You discipline yourself to concentrate on the way an arm will move, the turn of your head, and the stretch of your back.

Concentrate on your spacial environment and its effect on your program. Do not get "lost in space." Feel the boundaries of the rink, the distance of the walls and the ceiling. There are places within these boundaries toward which you want your gestures to be directed. Your focus may be toward or away from a point in your surroundings, but each gesture should have a direction; it should never appear to be floundering in space.

When executing your program, it is important to consider the space around you. Movements that look large and strong in a small room will look weaker and smaller on the ice. Your gestures will look larger during a practice session with many skaters filling the space around you, than when you are skating alone on the ice in an empty space. The relationship of your body to the surrounding space changes according to how the space is filled, and the difference can be dramatic. You must constantly discipline yourself and concentrate on extending your movements and making your designs clear enough to be seen over the vast amount of empty space. As an artist, you are making pictures for other people to look at. These pictures have to have significance because they are moving and are only there for an instant. When your program is over, you want your audience to carry these strong and beautiful images away with them.

Another point of concentration is learning to develop an inner focus: concentrating on the dramatic and emotional aspect of who you are and who you are relating to while skating. When you have trained your body in the language of expression, you will want to practice concentrating deeply within yourself until you reach the point where you are unaware of people watching you, or what other skaters are doing. When

you are intensely concentrating, your program becomes a part of you and you can give of yourself, communicating your feelings to the audience through your outward physical moves. When this happens, the audience is put in a position of sharing what you feel and is no longer in a passive role of just watching you skate. Instead, they are feeling something too. It is as if they have become a participant in your program and feel a part of your creative endeavor.

It is during times like this that large masses of people will rise to their feet to give a standing ovation to the skater. When your inner focus is working properly and a connection with the audience is successful, you achieve the ultimate in artistic satisfaction. It makes all the hard work and the many hours of practice seem insignificant in the face of the overwhelming glory of that moment.

I had the occasion to observe this type of artistic development during the years 1975, 1976, 1977, and 1978 while working with Wendy Burge as her choreographer and artistic coach. I watched her perfect the connection of emotional gesture between her inner and outer self through many hours of self-discipline and training. This culminated in her winning the long freestyle program at the United States Nationals in Hartford, Connecticut, in 1977 to a standing ovation; the bronze medal for freestyle at the World Figure Skating Championships in Tokyo, Japan; and the World's Professional Championship title in Jaca, Spain, that same year. As a professional show skater at this writing, Wendy still maintains this same exciting connection with her audiences whenever she skates.

CONFIDENCE

It is important that you look confident when you skate. People become uncomfortable watching a skater who looks unsure, weak, or negative in any way. Eliminate positions of the torso, limbs, and head that give this impression, such as the head down, shoulders forward, arms too low, chest caved in, and incomplete limb extensions.

If you skate with confidence, then your audience will believe in what you do. The best way to gain confidence is by knowing

Fig. 38.
Wendy Burge, Freestyle Bronze Medalist in 1977 World Figure
Skating Competition, 1977 World Professional Champion, and
Star of Ice Capades, working with Ricky Harris.

your work well. Do not risk waiting until the day of performance to display your expressive movements. They must be
rehearsed to give you confidence. The face is a very important,
expressive part of the body, and a variety of facial expressions
should be practiced in order to get the proper muscular response. If this is done sufficiently, then in performance you
will not have to think about it and the facial muscles will
respond automatically, resulting in what will be a spontaneous
look. I cannot emphasize enough the practice of facial expression.

I had one student, a child of ten years, who always looked
as if she were crying when she was skating. When she did try

to smile, it turned into a very plastic look. In order for her to acquire a pleasant expression on her face, one that would make her look like she was enjoying what she was doing, I gave her certain words to memorize to be said at key places in her program. On the landing of a jump, she said "wow," "say," or "oh boy." Coming out of a spin, her words were "hi," "good," or "great." When she was in a stroking pattern, I had her say things like, "This is fun." She said these words out loud for a while, and after several weeks I asked her just to think them. When she did, her expression still retained the expressive quality and relaxed look that she had while saying them out loud. I also observed that her body seemed to react positively to these exercises, and added to her new confident look. The words that you use can be key words from the story you have written about your program, as they will help you to maintain the characterization you wish to portray.

You will have more confidence if you practice the way you want your hands to look and feel. Be sure that energy flows out to the fingertips or you may get a "crippled" look. Change hand positions according to what the rest of the body is doing. A flat, flexed hand throughout a program becomes not only monotonous, but annoying. Keep the tension out of your hands and don't form fists. Test them by letting them hang loosely and relaxed at your sides, then lift them by moving your upper arms first.

Confidence is one of the main ingredients of style. The proof of your individual style will come when other skaters copy you. It is then that you know you have developed something unique. Never be angry or upset when this happens. It is a high compliment to you. At the same time, do not be afraid to be criticized. Criticism is a part of growth. You grow from your successes and your failures. Developing style means researching creativity, and originality will always be admired and envied. Even when you are given movements by your coach or choreographer, try to put into that movement your own individuality, injecting into it your personal style so that it becomes identifiable with you.

Make your entrance onto the ice with a feeling of great

confidence. Practice going onto the ice and to your starting place with smooth flowing strokes. A high stretch of your free leg as you approach it will enhance your look. Come to a smooth, efficient stop and, without shuffling your feet, immediately take your beginning pose. Do not fuss with your costume or your hair, and present yourself with a pleasant expression and smile.

When you have completed your program, a bow or acknowledgment to the judges and audience is in order. Bows must be practiced, as that is the time when you are tired and liable to lose balance or control. Experiment until you find just the right bow or gesture that suits your body, personality, and current costume and program.

A word of caution: consider that you are still "on stage" until you are off the ice. No matter how you skated your program, leave the ice with your head up, your body tall, and a calm face. Remember, this is still a competitive sport, and sportsmanlike behavior is necessary for a good reputation. If you need to vent your emotions, quickly go somewhere private and do so, away from the eyes of judges and audience.

PREPARING FOR COMPETITION

Preparing yourself properly for competition will add tremendously to your confidence. The skater who performs well at competition, and who exhibits the self-confidence and discipline which comes from proper training, is the skater who knows exactly what to do and precisely when to do it. Make a list that will help you check off all the things that you want to remember to do before a competition. The following is a typical example:

Competition Notes

A. Costumes

    1.   Two skating outfits (one for figures and one for freestyle) ready at least one week before competition. a. Material, color, and pattern to be approved by your professional.

b. Test your costumes by skating in them at least once.

2. Ladies, have an extra pair of tights ready to take with you in case of runs or tears.

3. A flesh-colored leotard, or one of the same color as the costume, available in case of cold weather or early morning.

4. A close-fitting sweater in a matching or complementary color for warm-up.

B. Skates

1. Sharpen skates no less than two weeks before competition.

2. Put in new laces several days before competition.

3. Carry an extra pair of laces.

4. Polish boots.

C. Bring records and tapes

D. Hair

1. Discuss your contemplated hairstyle with your coach several weeks before competition.

2. Make haircut appointment, if needed.

E. Arrange hotel accommodations well in advance.

F. Have two lists of your skating time schedules.

G. Arrive at least one hour before your event.

H. Register yourself and your music as you arrive.

I. Check in with your professional on arrival.

J. Do a good warm-up with or without supervision. (Refer to Chapter 12.)

K. Socialize *after* you have competed. Use any time you have left to concentrate on going over your program in your mind quietly and alone.

PART THREE

ADDITIONAL TRAINING ASPECTS

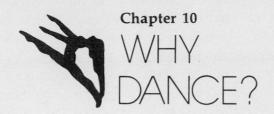

Chapter 10

WHY DANCE?

Painter's art is two dimensional. Sculptor's art is three dimensional. Dancer's art is fourth dimensional, embracing space and time.

—Nico Charisse

Since ice skating has taken a serious step toward being not only an athletic event, but also an artistic art form, the stylistic approach becomes one of great importance. To help skaters achieve an artistic style, off-ice dance classes are of great benefit. It is unsatisfactory to perform double and triple jumps and intricate spins without the continuity of beautiful transitions and forms between these maneuvers.

There are always a few skaters who seem to arrive at some personal style and line without formal training in a dance school. These few skaters have a natural charisma in performance. It seems evident, however, that along the way they have had contact with a dance teacher either on or off the ice, who has helped instill some idea of style into their performance. I can't help but feel that these very special people could certainly have doubled their artistic output with a consistent long-range program of academic dance training.

Classical ballet, modern dance, and jazz are the three important dance styles in western theatrical dancing. Ballet evolved over the past three centuries in Europe and is generally considered to be the best foundation for dance, with a scientific method of preparing the body to move. Today, ballet, modern, and jazz classes all teach techniques that involve proper alignment and body control, which can solve many skating problems.

Learning to control the pelvis, for example, is necessary for balance and control in skating. "Pinching the buttocks," and feeling those muscles wrap around from front to back, can do wonders for many skating moves. Dance classes teach the control of the pelvis as well as the complete use of all the muscles of the body.

Another important function of dance training is the development of a well-turned-out leg. This means that, through exercise, the leg will develop a greater amount of rotation in the hip socket. Do not confuse turning the hip out with turning the leg out. Always turning the hip out can lead to trouble in properly performing some skating moves. A leg that is not turned out will, when doing a spiral, an attitude, a camel spin, or a spread eagle, create an unattractive line in space. The spread eagle must come from the legs turned out in the hip sockets. If you force the spread eagle by pronating the feet, you will probably always have your bottom sticking out in the back and will never be able to develop the beautiful line of this exciting move.

The use of the knees in skating is very important. As muscles provide the greater part of the stability of the knee, they must be strengthened, particularly the quadriceps (see Fig. 39). One of the best ways to strengthen the quadriceps is by doing pliés (ballet knee bends).

Consistent repetition of pliés in dance classes also teaches the correct placement of the knees in relation to the toes. The knees and toes must always point in the same direction. If your knee points to the inside of the toe, you will find the weight pulling to an inside edge, which may cause problems in landing jumps. Dance teachers are trained to watch for problems such as this and correct them early enough to avoid a lasting bad habit.

Skaters who experience fear and anxiety in the practice of

Fig. 39.

Quadriceps
muscles

jumping skills usually hold their bodies in ways that express their emotions: tense muscles, raised shoulders, head down, and contracted middle. If this is repeated over a period of time, the muscles that are used in this particular way get set and a habit pattern is established. If you work on jumps, spins, or any technical move long enough, you will eventually lose the fear and build the strength and coordination to accomplish them. Using dance classes as a guide to understanding the structure of the body and the way the muscles work to build coordination, strength, and good posture, is a shortcut toward your skating goals.

Studying dance teaches you discipline of the mind as well as the body. Learning and practicing steps helps develop concentration for intricate footwork. I have found that those who study jazz and tap consistently improve their ability for footwork. As soon as you move into the structure of dancing, you are moving into an enormous depth of experience. From that dance experience you can take those moves and concepts which are most profitable to you.

The correct teaching of dance not only helps you develop balance and equilibrium, but offers an emotional response as well. Expressive thoughts can be turned into beautiful movements. By constantly working in rhythm, you will learn to move within the boundaries of time without conscious effort. This will eventually make you more graceful because the correct timing in using muscular power for a given act becomes a habit. You will then be using instinctive body movements, without effort, to produce rhythm and beauty.

Arts do not grow in isolation, but are influenced by common trends and by each other. Changes in the art forms of painting, art, sculpture, architecture, music, and poetry are very obvious in their written forms and visual images. With television and film exposure, changes in skating and dance forms can easily be seen. Changes in dance forms will affect the way skating progresses as an art form. If you train your body in the skills of dance styles, you will be able to adapt these changes into your work.

The only way that dance classes would be harmful to a skater is if they were taught incorrectly. It is the responsibility of your coach, your parents, and yourself to investigate thoroughly the various dance schools in your area, and to educate yourself as to what is good teaching and what is incorrect teaching. It just takes a little time and patience and is well worth the effort when you see the results. Do not hesitate to ask questions and compare. When you visit a school, watch beginning and intermediate as well as advanced classes. Every good dance class strives to accomplish the following:

> To stretch
> To strengthen
> To define line and form
> To coordinate

These four components also apply to skating.

Dance classes provide properly supervised stretching of the tendons. Tendons attach the muscles to the bones, and stretching them increases the range of motion of the parts to which they are attached. Stretching should never be done violently or in a jerky manner. Sudden and intense stretching can tear and weaken muscle tissue.

Always allow yourself enough time to stretch consistently and gradually. As you get more limber, the dance teacher will increase stretching, until your muscles become elastic and supple. Elasticity and flexibility are important aspects in skating. Stretching not only causes limberness in the muscles, but also develops strength. Strong muscles are needed to hold a leg up, completely stretched out in a spiral or a camel spin. The same theory applies to the muscles used to hold your arms up and your shoulders down.

Dance unites content, form, and technique:

Content —is the inner experience which the movement expresses. It is the feeling.

Form —is the outward perceptible aspect of the experience. The organic outgrowth of the content.

Technique —is the means of perfecting the form.

Everything that you learn in a dance class can be used on the ice. Even if a movement from the floor cannot be done technically on the ice, the essence of the move can be used.

Dance exercises, when done consistently, produce a responsive, coordinated body, ready and able to perform anything that your mind desires to express. When you have mastered the principles of movement, they can be applied instantly, and without conscious thought, to any problem of expression or abstract movement. With the proper disciplined background, you will be able to communicate a powerful, inner essence to your audience.

Fig. 40.
Ballet class at the Ricky Harris Dance Studio. From left to right: Karen Sefton, Robin Loveland, Tracy Rowe, Vikki Jacque, Joan Campbell, and Allan Gonzales. Photographer: Paul Piazzese

Fig. 41.
Ballet class at
the Ricky
Harris Dance
Studio. From
left to right:
Andrea Key,
Patricia Neske,
Laura La Riva,
Michelle
Mantelino, Lori
Koshi, Tracy
Rowe.
Photographer:
Paul Piazzese

Fig. 42.
Ballet class at the Ricky Harris Dance Studio. Front to back:
Laura La Riva, Patricia Neske, Lori Koshi, Yvonne Gutierrez,
Paige Korenich, and Sue Packard. Photographer: Paul Piazzese

Chapter 11

THE FATIGUE FACTOR

Grace is efficiency of movement.
　　　　　　　　　—Delsarte

Fatigue is a common by-product of a physical activity. Among figure skaters, it often results from the way in which the body is used in daily activity and in performing skating skills. There are many factors that can cause fatigue among skaters; they are:

1. Poor body alignment

2. Inefficient movements

3. Anxiety

4. Improper breathing

5. Inefficient circulatory system

6. Improper warm-ups

7. Insufficient rest

8. Diet

BODY ALIGNMENT

One of the prime functions of muscles is to maintain the body in different moving and stationary positions against the pull of gravity. Poor posture habits and faulty breathing can cause groups of muscles in the thorax (the part of the body between the neck and the abdomen) to work incorrectly. This can alter the balance of the body and set up a reflex action in other muscles which will restrict your movements and cause fatigue. Therefore, correcting your body alignment is important not only in terms of body line and style, but also in endurance and the performance of figure-skating skills.

Place your head so that it is held directly at the top of your spine. It helps to think of your spine as beginning in your tailbone and ending at the top of your head. Keep your spine flexible so that you can create artistic expression, but free from abnormal curves and pressures. Balance all the body segments one on top of the other.

Body Alignment Check:

1. Stand sideways in front of a full-length mirror, feet slightly apart.

2. Straighten your legs, feeling your muscles lengthen.

3. Squeeze your buttocks together; do not push the pelvis forward, or release it backward.

4. Push your belly button to the back of your spine.

5. Lift your rib cage and chest.

6. Press down with your shoulders and back muscles.

7. Keep your neck in line with your back. Imagine a line from the tailbone to the top of the head.

8. Keep your chin in a normal position, not too high, not too low.

9. Feel the top of your head reaching for the ceiling.

After practicing your body alignment, observe your image in the mirror, close your eyes, and put yourself in the same position. Open your eyes and make any necessary corrections. Continue doing this until you can place yourself in the proper body alignment without looking.

In landing jumps, much emphasis is placed on the "checkout" position. Here again, keep the spine and surrounding body segments in line. Too many times there is an exaggerated protruding chest, causing the chin to pull down, the back to overarch, and the arms to press unnaturally back of the shoulders. In this position it is difficult to raise the free leg off the ice to a proper height.

Upon landing, keep your torso slightly inclined forward over the hips and the skating knee, your spine straight, and your arms out to the side from the shoulders (see Figure 43). In this position, landings can be made with no strain to the body. This will lessen fatigue and free your leg so it can rise to an attractive height. Your head will look more natural and your neck long, resulting in a more artistic appearance. Later on, when this body position becomes natural to you, you will be able to use different arm positions for your landings.

INEFFICIENT MOVEMENTS

Many fatigue problems are caused by inefficient movements that become habitual. Change these habits by redirecting your energies. Good habits can be developed through concentrated thought and repetition of exercises, as in the case of stroking. Improper stroking habits result in wasteful energy and unnecessary fatigue for the skater. This can be remedied by observing the proper stroking procedures as listed in Chapter 13.

ANXIETY

Anxiety can cause hypertension, resulting in a rigid and/or raised shoulder area. This may cause tension in the upper spine and neck. Tightening in any one area of the spine or chest may

produce misa-
lignment in the
entire body, es-
pecially in the
vertebral column.

1. Stand up!

2. Tighten all
the muscles of
the upper torso
and head.

3. Hold for
one minute.

You now real-
ize how exhaust-
ing it can be to
tighten the mus-
cles in your
body. Be aware
of this condition
and practice ten-
sion and relaxa-
tion exercises.
Muscle relaxa-
tion is important
to remedy fatigue and restore elasticity and flexibility.

Fig. 43.
Jump landing position.

Tension-relieving Exercises
Head Circles. Stand with feet slightly apart, arms and hands
relaxed by your sides, head in a normal position facing front.

Count 1: Move head so the right ear drops in a direct line
over the right shoulder.

Count 2: Roll the head so it drops backward.

Count 3: Move the head so that the left ear drops in a direct line over the left shoulder.

Count 4: Roll the head so it drops completely forward and the chin is directly over the center of the chest.

The four counts should be done in a continuous movement. Repeat four times to the right and four times to the left.

Shoulder Circles. Use same stance as for head circles.

Count 1: Move both shoulders forward.

Count 2: Lift shoulders up.

Count 3: Move shoulders to the back.

Count 4: Drop shoulders to normal position.

Do this exercise in a continuous movement four times, then reverse.

Stretch and Relaxation Exercises
Arm and Rib Cage Stretch. Stand straight, feet apart.

Count 1: Reach up with right hand high above head, bending right knee, left leg straight, left hip out.

Count 2: Reach with left hand high above head, bending left knee, right leg straight, right hip out.

Count 3: Repeat count 1.

Count 4: Repeat count 2.

Counts 5,6,7: Same as counts 1,2,3, except that you rise high on the balls of the feet, keeping knees straight.

Count 8: Relax body in a quick slump all the way down to the floor, letting knees bend.

Immediately rise and start exercise again. Repeat four times.

Complete Body Stretches. Start with the body completely relaxed down to the floor, slumped forward, knees bent, feet slightly apart, head resting on chest.

Counts 1 to 8: Start stretching up slowly beginning with the ankles, knees, thighs, hips, abdomen, waist, rib cage, shoulders, and head in succession. Reach an upright tense position by the count of 8. Arms are at sides, fingers stretched and apart.

Counts 9 to 16: Start down by relaxing head first, then shoulders, rib cage, waist, abdomen, hips, thighs, knees, ankles in succession until you are back in your starting position, completely relaxed.

Do exercise in 8 counts twice, 6 counts twice, 4 counts twice, 2 counts four times, and 1 count eight times. At the last count, stand for a moment in the extreme tense position before relaxing.

It is not unusual for skaters to overwork their bodies. Overtaxed muscles become tense with strain; underused ones, tense from neglect. Both situations cause fatigue. Tension, stretch, and relaxation exercises before and after practice and competition can alleviate some of this condition.

BREATHING

A skater needs a well-conditioned cardiovascular system to provide the stamina required for the competitive or professional program. Correct breathing implies control of the diaphragm and should play an important part in skating training. Incorrect breathing results in shortness of breath and bad circulation. To breathe correctly is to breathe through the nose.

Besides filtering the air, breathing through the nose warms the air as it passes through the nasal passages.

The body's source of oxygen is the air we breathe. It is transported by the blood to the tissue cells. The waste product of carbon dioxide in the tissues is carried by the blood through the lungs and exhaled out of the body. Breathing is increased during physical exercise. There are three different ways to breathe:

1. Using the upper lungs. This is shallow breathing and is least efficient.

2. Through the middle lung, using a little of the abdomen.

3. Using the lower abdomen, or diaphragm. This is most efficient.

When you inhale correctly, there is a downward action of the diaphragm, and the abdominal wall draws back. The rib cage should expand and contract with each breath.

Breathing Exercises

Standing. Put your hands on your rib cage, elbows out to the sides. Breathe through your nose for 4 counts, feeling your rib cage separate and abdominal wall retract. Exhale through your mouth for 4 counts, feeling the rib cage draw together. Repeat this 4 times, gradually increasing daily to ten times.

Walking. Keep your mouth slightly open. Breathe through your nose and exhale through your mouth while walking around a room. Keep the breathing even and rhythmical as you begin to improvise arm movements while you are walking.

Skating. Using your rhythmical breathing pattern in above exercise, go through some stroking patterns on the ice, improvising arm movements.

It is hard to breathe evenly during strenuous skating, but breathing patterns can be used to help accomplish the compulsory skating moves. For example, you could make a complete exhalation on the preparation to a jump, then take a deep inhalation on takeoff (holding the breath until the landing), then exhale on the landing. This develops control and lessens fatigue.

Forming good breathing patterns is well worth the effort when you find yourself not tiring so easily. When your body becomes tense, help it relax by practicing the deep-breathing exercises.

CIRCULATORY SYSTEM

It is important that the body maintain a good circulatory system as an aid in reducing fatigue. You can do this by following a daily regimen of conditioning exercises. The reason for this is that the muscles play an important part in the circulation of the blood through our bodies. The action of the heart is to pump blood, but the action of our muscles determines how much blood gets to any part of the body. Muscles act as relay pumps, increasing blood flow to their local parts. Skaters who take dance classes are conditioning their bodies.

WARM-UPS

There is a great misconception among ice skaters as to what "warming up" really means. Basically it means increasing the body temperature. In order to clearly define the proper warm-up exercises that will help prevent injury, unnecessary soreness, and fatigue; and encourage greater efficiency as a skater, I have devoted an entire chapter to this subject. Please refer to Chapter 12.

REST AND DIET

The following is a list of conditions that would apply to the reduction of fatigue for skaters:

1. Rest with legs up after working for long periods of time. A good position is to lie down on the floor on your back

(keeping warm) with your derriere (buttocks) close to the wall and your legs up, feet touching the wall.

2. Get eight hours of sleep in a comfortable bed, in a dark, quiet, and cool room.

3. Eat a nutritious diet containing the essential elements that maintain normal and attractive body weight. Being just three pounds over normal weight can cause excess fatigue. A distended stomach may interfere with the action of the heart during heavy exercise and restrict its blood flow. The consequent restriction of blood flow through the heart ultimately affects endurance and fatigue. Allow enough time after meals for digestion before actively skating.

4. Never use drugs to allay sensations of fatigue.

5. Follow exposure to extreme fatigue in very high altitudes by ample periods of rest to promote full recovery.

It is your responsibility, ultimately, to view your body as an instrument, and to learn to use it with ease, grace, flexibility, and freedom from strain, thereby lessening fatigue.

Chapter 12

WARMING UP

The world is moving so fast these days that the man who says it can't be done is generally interrupted by someone doing it.

—Elbert Hubbard

Warming up is a subject that evokes interest and controversy on the part of everyone involved in skating. The process of warming up is generally accepted by almost all athletes, coaches, and dancers, but there are many opinions on how this should be done. Different methods seem to work for different people, as each body varies in its metabolism. Metabolism is the process by which nourishment and waste products are handled in the body, resulting in the use and release of energy.

It is important to know your body and what type of warm-up will work for you. I know of one famous dancer who felt best when given a thorough nonballetic warm-up. This was followed by a series of brief, more traditional ballet exercises before performing. Some athletes seem to need longer warm-up periods than others, and some skaters claim not to need a warm-up at all!

I find it quite strange that skaters will make a big point of doing off-ice exercises before a competition, yet feel it is unimportant before their daily practice. Many skaters think they are warming up when they go to the rail and perform a series of stretching exercises before they skate, but . . .

Stretching is not warming up!

Stretching is increasing flexibility, making the muscles longer and more elastic.

PHYSICAL RESPONSES TO WARMING UP

Warming up means raising your body temperature through heating your blood and muscles. Your blood circulation is like a transportation system, running all through your body, picking up and carrying supplies that nourish your cells. These supplies, which turn into energy, are picked up from the liver and stomach, and transported through veins and arteries to your muscles. At the same time, the blood picks up waste products and carries them out of the body through the kidneys and lungs.

Warm-up exercises make your blood pump faster and, as a result, your muscles get more supplies and get rid of waste products faster. This allows the muscles to work harder, thus increasing your skating capacity.

When your blood pumps faster, your heart rate rises and all your reactions are faster and more efficient. This is because nerve messages travel faster at higher temperatures. The increased blood flow also improves lung circulation.

EQUILIBRIUM

Equilibrium is a state of balance between two opposite forces, resulting in no change in the state of the body.

Your sense of balance comes from the position of your equilibrium equipment, which affects the muscles automatically. If your muscles do not respond fast enough, you will give the impression of insecurity. The main idea is to feel a vertical line through 95 percent of your program, except for the times when you are doing camel spins, arabians, and spirals. But even then you have to have a center of balance.

Muscles are stiff and slow when they are not warmed up. This disturbs your equilibrium. Warmed muscles will respond automatically to equilibrium, without your having to think about it. It is more reasonable then, to warm up your body, and subsequently your equilibrium, on the floor before you start to disturb your equilibrium equipment with complicated spins and multiple revolution jumps on the ice.

BASIC STEPS OF A WARM-UP

1. Accelerate your blood circulation and increase your heart rate. This also accelerates your metabolism.

2. Warm up your muscles slowly in order of their size: the legs and buttocks, the back, arms and shoulders, stomach, and the twisting muscles of the torso.

DAILY WARM-UPS

The problem is finding the time to do a warm-up before freestyle. Coaches know that it is beneficial, yet the way ice time is arranged, there are only a few minutes between patch and freestyle. They are anxious for their skaters to get on the ice to take full advantage of the ice time. Besides, they want to be sure to get all of their scheduled lessons fitted into the allotted time.

Parents get upset when their children do not get on the ice right away, as they are paying for that time. Many feel it is "wasted" when the skater spends it on exercise on the floor. But if you are seriously interested in increasing your speed and getting more efficiency from your muscles by doing a warm-up before freestyle, here are some suggestions on how to do it:

1. Leave the patch two minutes before it is over. I suggest discussing this with your coach so that he/she will have an understanding of what you are trying to accomplish. The benefits derived will far outweigh the loss of the two minutes of patch.

2. Take the two minutes out of the beginning of your freestyle period instead of patch. You will find that you will make up these two minutes by being better prepared for the ice and, as a result, you will accomplish more work with greater efficiency.

3. Do not socialize with anyone. Quickly remove your figure boots. Put on tennis shoes or something equally suitable and you are ready for a *two-minute warm-up.*

TWO-MINUTE WARM-UP

The following warm-up suggestions are for skaters who have no special physical problems, and who need guidelines on how to improve their skating capacity through floor warm-ups.

*1. **Running in Place.*** 25 seconds. (Accelerates heart rate.) Run as fast as you can in place, lifting your knees high each time you step.

Relax and Breathe for 5 seconds, inhaling through your nose and exhaling through your mouth. At the same time, shake your hands and feet.

*2. **Full Knee-bends.*** 10 seconds. (For legs and buttocks.) Stand with feet in a parallel position about five inches apart. Keeping your heels on the floor, and with arms straight ahead, bend all the way down and then back up again (see Fig. 44). Do this eight times.

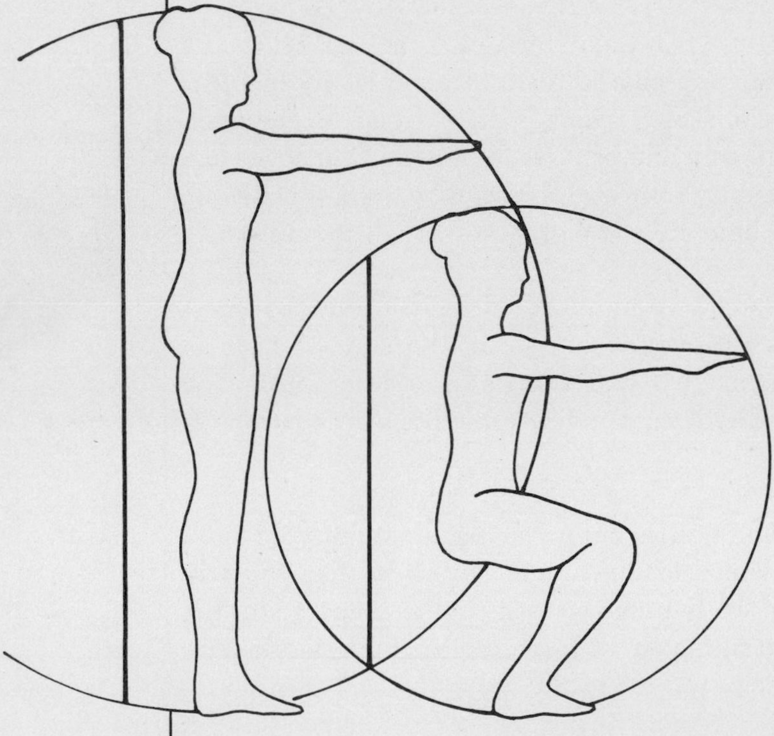

Relax and breathe for 5 seconds.

*3. **Bend-overs.*** 15 seconds. (For the back.) Standing with feet parallel, extend your

Fig. 44.
Full knee-bends from two-minute warm-up.

arms straight above your head. Bend the whole torso forward in one piece from the hips to a position parallel to the floor. The back does not bend. Still maintaining the straight spine, bring your whole torso back to starting position (see Fig. 45). Keep your stomach pulled in through this exercise. Do this eight times.

Relax and breathe for 5 seconds.

4. *Push-aways.* 10 seconds. (For shoulders and arms.) Stand an arm's distance away from a wall. Place hands on

Fig. 45.
Bend-overs from two-minute warm-up.

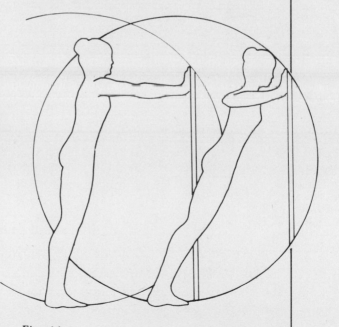

Fig. 46.
Push-aways from two-minute warm-up.

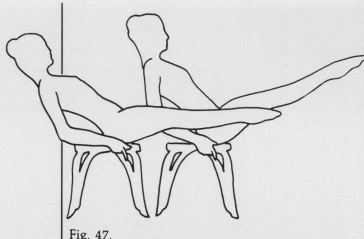

Fig. 47.
Leg and torso raise from two-minute warm-up.

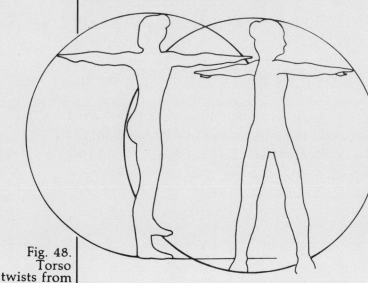

Fig. 48.
Torso
twists from
two-minute
warm-up.

the wall directly in front of you, bending the elbows (see Fig. 46). Push away eight times.

Relax and breathe for 5 seconds.

5. Leg and Torso Raise. 10 seconds. (For the stomach).
Balance your tailbone on a chair or bench, supporting yourself with your hands on the chair. Raise your torso and legs together and return, six times (see Fig. 47).

Relax and breathe for 5 seconds.

6. Torso Twists. 10 seconds. (For lower back.)
Stand with feet parallel, arms straight out to sides. Swinging the body from above the hips, twist as far as possible side to side, eight times. (see Fig. 48).

7. Slow Jogging (warming down). 10 seconds.

Relax and breathe for 5 seconds.

This schedule of a two-minute warm-up is very intensive, and requires a certain level of physical qualities. If you are not in good physical condition, it may be a little hard on you and make your freestyle a bit difficult for a few weeks. Do not get discouraged. Remain patient and give yourself at least three weeks to adjust to this new training schedule. You will then see the advantage of it.

A good time to start your new warm-up schedule is right after you have finished your competitive season. Or you may want to start in the summer before your important competitions begin in the fall. This will give you enough time to get used to it. I suggest that you start gradually. Do half of the suggested exercises at first. Instead of running in place for 25 seconds, run for 15 seconds. Instead of doing eight knee-bends, do four. Until you get used to this schedule, go at a slower pace with bigger intervals for breathing and relaxing.

Do not confuse this type of warm-up with exercises for style, strength, endurance, and flexibility, although it will help. There are different exercises for those that can be accomplished either through dance classes, or through other off-ice maneuvers. The two-minute warm-up before freestyle greatly accelerates the heart rate and blood flow to the muscles, making them more stable and elastic. Warming up helps prevent injury when circulation increases and lubrication occurs around the main joints which work in skating.

The two minutes that you take off from either your patch or your freestyle will not be lost completely. You will save about ten minutes of ice time because you will be physically warmed up, instead of trying to warm up on the ice and struggling through your first few jumps. You will gain two or three minutes in putting on your skates because you will be breathing so hard, you will not have any desire to talk. The warm-up will make your hands and fingers move faster and you will get your skates on quicker.

AFTER WARM-UP

Start your ice practice with some stroking. By stroking, you are warming up your equilibrium equipment and the coordination mechanism of your muscles to adjust to the conditions of the ice, and the size of the rink. After stroking, go over to the rail and stretch. There is less possibility now of overstretching and hurting your muscles.

I conducted an experiment once for several months with a ten-year-old skater. She had her first lesson with me on afternoon sessions once or twice a week. I asked her not to go on the ice until she had completed a warm-up on the floor that I had instructed her to do. She got to the rink before freestyle started and did the warm-up in ten minutes. When she came on the ice, she was not allowed to stroke, stretch, or do anything other than put her record on and go through her program. Within a month, she was doing perfect programs almost every time with this schedule. The hardest part was getting the idea out of her head that she would not be able to land a jump in her program unless she had warmed it up on the ice.

As I said, this was an experiment, and I do not advise doing this as a general practice.

COMPETITIVE WARM-UP

Before a competition, your warm-up should be more thorough —lasting at least twenty minutes. Do this warm-up in practice clothes, as you will perspire. If you do not, you did not get much out of it, and you are not warmed up.

When you go on the ice for a warm-up at a competition, you cannot go over to the rail to stretch because you need to use that time more effectively. Therefore, besides general warm-up exercises, it is advisable also to stretch off-ice before putting on your skates.

The main purpose of this warm-up is to involve the muscles

in work, but not get them overtired. There will be some individual differences in the quantity of the warm-up for different test levels. Skaters in lower test levels are not in as good physical shape, so they would do fewer exercises, fewer repetitions, with less intensity, so as not to get too tired before getting on the ice.

LENGTH AND INTENSITY OF WARM-UP FOR COMPETITION

Start approximately one hour before you are to skate, and break up the hour in the following manner:

Warm-up exercises with breathing and relaxing	15 min.
Change into costume (no skates)	15 min.
Stretching exercises	10 min.
Put on skates	5 min.
"Stay loose" (walking around, shaking hands and feet; thinking about your program)	15 min.

Use the exercises from the two-minute daily warm-up as a base from which to work. Your intensity depends on your level of skating, and you have more time now to add exercises that are more closely related to your program. Be sure to include the breathing and relaxing breaks. Other warm-up exercises you can do are:

1. Jumping jacks

2. Bench stepping

3. Skipping rope

4. Jazz steps

For the stretching, use exercises that stretch the muscles that have to work on the ice for things like:

1. Spirals

2. Laybacks

3. Split jumps

4. Camel spins

5. Sit spins

Be very careful of any exercises that involve "bobbing," as this can lead to injuries of connective tissues in the "all-out" effort of your competitive program. It is possible to injure yourself, or set yourself up for injury in an area that you have stretched with this type of exercise.

When working on flexibility, I highly recommend very slow stretches, and always after warming up your muscles.

In the 1979 World competition in Vienna, everyone was amazed to watch Jan Hoffman, the East German Men's Champion, who warmed up for a half hour before getting on the ice. During the ice warm-up, when the other skaters were just on the single axel, he was already doing his triple lutz. It gave him more time to feel the ice; to feel the technique of the jump; to feel more secure and not limited by those six minutes of the warm-up. Psychologically, he seemed really quiet and confident.

STAYING LOOSE

After your warm-up and stretching, when you have your boots on and are ready to go, spend any remaining time moving around slowly. Move just enough to keep those warmed muscles on the same level. Shake your hands and feet to keep them relaxed. Use breathing patterns to help you keep calm. Then go out and skate your best!

Chapter 13

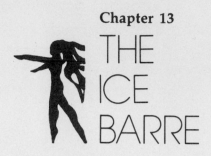THE ICE BARRE

Only those who have the patience to do simple things perfectly, ever acquire the skill to do difficult things easily.

—Johann C. Schiller

Traditionally, every ballet class begins with a barre that lasts from thirty to forty minutes, depending on the length of the entire class. The barre is a series of ballet exercises performed with one hand holding onto a bar, generally of wood, fixed to a wall of a practice room. The dancer uses the bar as support to keep balance.

PURPOSE OF A BALLET BARRE

Barre exercises are organized in a manner to develop muscular strength, flexibility and stretch, coordination, turnout, and line and form. These exercises are very important as they are the essence of everything that the dancer does on the floor in center work. They are to dancing what scales are to the pianist.

PURPOSE OF THE ICE BARRE

The ice barre is a series of stroking exercises that I have developed, incorporating some of the arabesque positions from ballet that can be used in skating. The primary purpose of this ice barre is not speed, but the conditioning of the body. It helps to develop strong and smooth stroking, with stretched-out thrusts, flexibility, coordination, turnout, and certain basic designs in space that will define line and form. Stroking entirely for speed can be done separately, although you will be skating as fast as you can around the rink ends to give you the momentum to accomplish the two inside edge patterns going forward down the length of the ice. The daily practice of the ice barre will develop the muscle memory needed to fall into correct positions without conscious effort when skating your program.

ICE BARRE EXERCISES

Forward Stroking Counterclockwise (see Fig. 49).

a. As you crossover around the top and bottom curves of the rink, press your shoulders down and your back muscles together. Your arms will be shoulder level, right arm front, left arm back. Do not wiggle or bounce them up and down, or let them move in front of your shoulders. With hands relaxed but with wrists straight, feel the stretch in the upper arms. Turn your head to the left so you will be looking down the center of the rink rather than over your right shoulder.

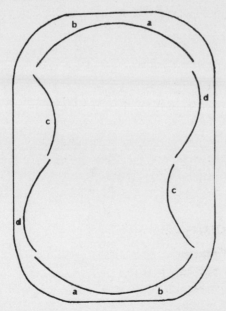

Fig. 49.
Ice pattern for forward stroking.

This gives you a better presentation. Hold your back up in line with your hips.

b. To crossover, stroke onto the left outside edge, keeping the knee well bent. As you cross the right foot over for the inside edge, replace the left knee with the right knee the same distance from the ice. This prevents the body from bouncing up and down with each stroke. At the moment of the crossover, the left leg thrusts in the direction of the outside of the ice curve (see Fig. 50a). Extend the free leg fully with each thrust. As the left foot comes together with the right to prepare for the next stroke, again match the left knee to the right knee (see Fig. 50b), stroking onto the left outside edge once again (see Fig. 50c). *Stay down on the knee.* Too much raising and lowering of the knees will cause a break in the flow of stroking. Do not push with your toe. Use the middle of the blade. Always lean into the center of the curve. A common fault is to have the top part of the body leaning outside the curve, taking you off a good inside edge of the crossed foot, and decreasing your speed. Keep the extended free leg close to the ice.

Fig. 50. Forward crossover (a) the thrust, (b) keeping knees same distance from the ice, (c) the stroke.

c. After crossovers around the curve, stroke onto an inside edge on the left foot, in the direction of the middle of the rink and curving toward the rail (see Fig. 49). Lift and extend the right leg in back (turned out from the hip) but slightly to the inside of the curve tracing. Keep your shoulders and hips square to the edge. Squeeze your buttocks together to hold this position securely. At the same time that you stroke onto the left inside edge, begin moving your right arm to a curved position in front of the right thigh. Without stopping, continue the movement up to the front in line with your chest, and extend it out to the side again (see Fig. 51). Keep your hands relaxed and start the movement from your upper arm. Follow the movements of your arm with your eyes and head.

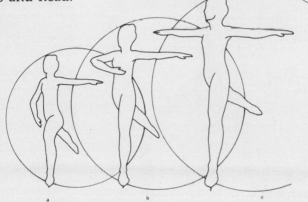

Fig. 51.
Arm and head movements for forward stroking on inside edges (a) arm low, (b) arm middle, (c) arm out to side with head following.

d. Repeat step c, reversing to a right inside edge using opposite arms. As you approach the end of the rink, the arms will have finished the movements and will be extended out to the sides, shoulder level. Keep your head turned to face down the center of the rink as your crossovers begin again around the curve.

After stroking three times around the rink following this pattern, reverse all directions and stroke clockwise.

Back Crossovers with First Arabesque. (Caution: Always look back to watch for skaters, unless you are on the ice alone;

then practice moving your head from front to back with the movement of the arms.)

1. Start back crossovers, counterclockwise, around the curve of the rink on the outside edge of your right foot (see Fig. 53). Cross your left foot over to an inside edge as the right leg thrusts and extends completely to the back and left in a crossed position (see Fig. 52). As in forward crossovers, stay

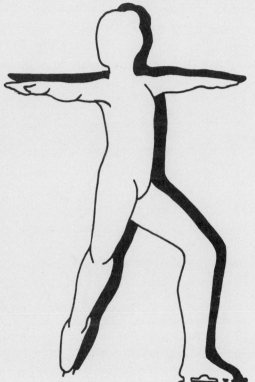

down on the knee and replace one with the other to prevent bobbing up and down. If you are careful to put your right foot down on a good outside edge, and crossover with an inside, you will eliminate the hip swaying action caused by reaching out with the right leg to an inside edge, and rolling over to the outside edge.

Fig. 52.
Back crossover.

Extend the arms fully at shoulder level with the head turned toward the center, as in Forward Stroking Counterclockwise.

2. As you approach the center of the figure eight ice pattern (see Fig. 53), come to the basic position. The basic position is both feet together, knees straight, arms down and curved, fingertips about one inch apart (see Fig. 54). Without pushing, move from the basic position into first arabesque position just by raising the leg. Going in this direction, you will be on your right leg with your left leg raised (see Fig. 55). Always lift the leg closest to where you are going. Your back is held upright from the waist, with your raised leg at right angles to your support leg. The raised leg is to be held in a turned-out position. Do not lift the hip to get your leg high. The correct daily stretching will eventually enable you to get your leg to the proper height.

Hold your shoulders square to the edge, with arms extended, right arm forward with hand slightly above eyes, and left arm sloping back. Both arms are in one line (see Fig. 55). The arm movement and the lift of the leg begin together and flow into position. Hold the first arabesque position until you are ready for the next crossovers.

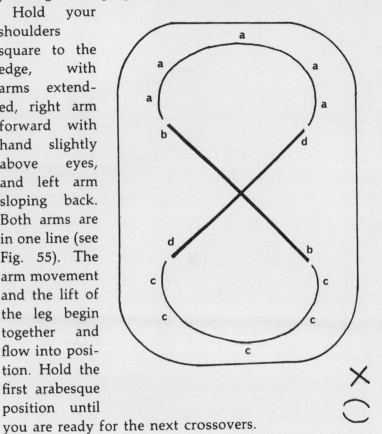

Fig. 53.
Ice pattern for back crossovers and arabesque positions.

arabesque patterns

crossovers

3. Repeat back crossovers, reversing feet, around the second lobe of the figure eight ice pattern (see Fig. 53c and d).

4. Come to basic position, then into first arabesque position, reversing arms and legs.

Back Crossovers with First Arabesque Plié (bent knee).
1. Repeat back crossovers around curves (see Fig. 53a and 53c).

2. Change from basic position to first arabesque with the support knee in plié going through center (see Fig. 56).

3&4. Repeat exercise on second lobe, reversing arms and legs.

Fig. 54. Basic position before arabesques in back stroking pattern.

Fig. 55. First arabesque position.

Back Crossovers in Second Arabesque.
1. Back crossovers around curves.

2. Basic position into second arabesque. Keep both knees straight. The forward arm is shoulder level and opposite to the supporting leg. The other arm extends out to the side (see Fig. 57a). As you hold second arabesque position, let your forward arm curve and move toward the back, while the other arm moves to the front, ending in first arabesque position (see Fig. 57b).

3 & 4. Reverse on second lobe.

Fig. 56.
First arabesque plié position.

Fig. 57.
(a) second arabesque position with straight knees.
(b) end in first arabesque position.

Back Crossovers with Second Arabesque Plié and Back-bend.

1. Back crossovers around curves.

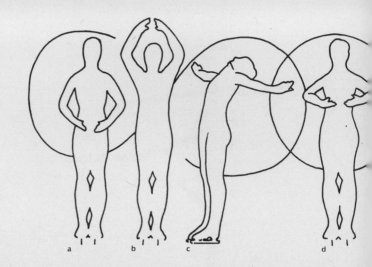

Fig. 58.
(a) basic position;
(b) arms move in
a circle above
head; (c) bend
back as arms
open;

2. Basic position (see Fig. 58a). Move curved arms to above head (see Fig. 58b). Bend back, extending arms to side (see Fig. 58c), as you ascend to an upright position. Continue arms into a circle in front of body (see Fig. 58d), and push into second arabesque with a plié of supporting leg (see Fig. 58e). Curve front arm and move it to the back, with both arms ending in first arabesque position (see Fig. 58f). These moves should be done in succession as one movement phrase, following pattern "b" in Figure 53.

3 &4. Reverse on second lobe.

Back Crossovers with Third Arabesque.
1. Back crossovers around curves.

2. Basic position into third arabesque (see Fig. 59a) with straight knees. The right arm is front and the hand is slightly above the eyes. The left arm is front at chest level, and is opposite to supporting leg.

Slowly turn left arm over so the palm faces up. Swing it down and up to the back as you end in first arabesque position (see Fig. 59b).

3&4. Reverse on second lobe.

e   f

(d) arms move in circle to front of body; (e) push into plié position; second arabesque (f) finish in first arabesque position.

Back Crossovers to Back Lunges (see Fig. 60).

. Back crossovers around curves.

. From basic position, extend leg into a back lunge. It is mportant to keep shoulders and hips square to the supporting leg. Practice back lunges very slowly at first. Flex foot nd lift leg to back, holding it up as the supporting knee ends down as far as possible. Keep arms extended out to ides as you place foot on the ice. When you rise from this osition, lift leg off the ice before you begin to rise.

&4. Repeat other lobe.

Fig. 59.
(a) third arabesque position (b) finish in first arabesque position

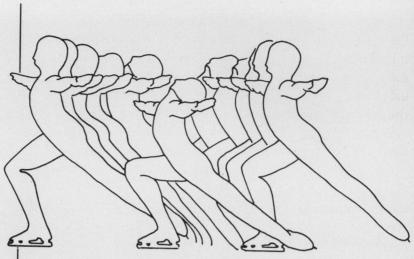

Fig. 60.
Back lunge.

ADVANCED WORK

1. Improvise different arm movements during forward and back crossovers around curves of rink.

This exercise is in addition to, not in place of, the out-stretched arms. The stretch of the arms is soon lost if not practiced continually.

2. Use mohawks, three turns, chainé turns, etc., with cross-overs.

3. Keep the pace even, but go as fast as you can.

4. During backbend in back crossovers with second ara-besque plié and backbend, balance on one leg, with the other one in a passé (foot pointed, with toe in line with and touch-ing the knee of the supporting leg).

5. Bend back during the lunges, with arms coming up in a circle over head.

CROSSOVERS IN CIRCLES

Practicing crossovers in a circle is helpful for improving stroking. Begin in slow motion, deliberately exaggerating every movement, until you feel stretched-out and solid. As you gradually build up speed, the circle will get larger. Remember that the strength of the stroke is in the thrust, not in the extension.

Stroking in rhythm will develop a sense of timing for each stroke. This is invaluable to the general flow of your skating.

Never feel that you have finally learned to stroke. As long as you are competing or performing, or have the desire to improve your skating, you should stroke. Correct stroking creates fluidity of movement, and develops the speed and strength necessary for the proper execution of your elements. Your whole program is enhanced by beautiful stroking.

Stroking meticulously daily will develop:

1. Strength in leg muscles.

2. Stretch in the leg.

3. A strong back.

4. Strength in the upper arm.

5. Timing and rhythm needed for entry into jumps.

6. Form and flow after completion of jumps and spins.

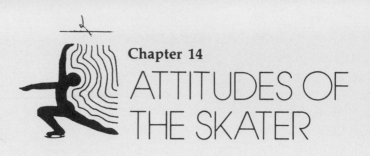

Chapter 14

ATTITUDES OF THE SKATER

To be a genuine individualist requires a great deal of strength and courage. It is never easy to chart new territory, to cross new frontiers, or to introduce subtle shadings to an established color.

—Toller Cranston

How do some skaters reach the top echelon in skating? As young students, they were with others who were given the same training by their coaches. Natural coordination and athleticism, as well as a built-in charisma, is to be taken into consideration, but this is not always the formula for ultimate success.

What seems to lead to success eventually is determining exactly what your goal is. You may have little ones along the way, but the important thing is to want something so badly that you can visualize it. Writing your goal down will help you define exactly what you want. After that, you must have the driving force toward the perfection of technique, and individuality of self-expression. Lastly, you must be willing to spend the time to make it happen through many hours of hard work.

Champions are not average people. They are superhuman beings. In addition to their conscious and subconscious minds, they have superconscious minds.

1. Conscious mind: It sees things as they appear to be, and implants both negative and positive reactions into the subconscious mind.

2. Subconscious mind: Its direction comes from the conscious mind and can be very powerful in both negative and positive ways.

3. Superconscious mind: It can visualize and fantasize things that seem to be out of reach for the average person, and make them happen. Instead of "should" it thinks "could." It thinks only in positives.

YOU CAN DEVELOP A SUPERCONSCIOUS MIND
Many times your mind will apprehend a principle, but your body does not seem able to apply and use the material which is so self-evident. But after continued practice, there will come the day when you will feel fulfillment and perfect application.

DISCIPLINE
Successful skaters are tough! By that I do not mean someone who is hard. Hard gives the connotation of being brittle. By tough I mean resilient and recuperative; having the ability to bounce back when the average skater has given up . . .

. . . to stroke one more time around the rink after everyone else has stopped.

. . . to fight for a landing, even when the jump is not quite right.

. . . to work for superb technique.

. . . to find your artistic potential and expand it to the utmost.

It takes as much discipline to be an artistic skater as it does to be a good technical skater. You need a regimen of training with no casual practices. There is enough time in every free-style session to devote part of it to your artistic training. If you eliminate a lot of social conversation, standing at the rail, or needlessly hanging around the record player, you will save at least ten or fifteen minutes that you can devote to your artistic practice. It is more profitable to use time and energy toward a

particular end so that time and energy become the means. You will benefit from this type of discipline if you are prepared to accept it.

Constantly stretch your mind as well as your body, to far-reaching, deep, intellectual, and creative approaches to your work. Do not just look at things, but *see* them. Do not just listen, but *hear.* You can get inspiration from reading, seeing dance concerts, going to sculpture and art exhibits. Being exposed to all visual arts will expand your vision and better fulfill your ambition to be a creative and artistic performer.

CREATIVE TRAITS

There are different degrees of creativity. Under the right circumstances, and with a disciplined approach, you can reach the highest levels of creativity. Striving for creativity develops a respect for individuality. It does not mean throwing out all the old ways of doing things. Rather, it means experimenting with new approaches, perhaps better and quicker ways to gain results.

Creative people have certain traits that are recognizable:

1. An open mind
   a. They have an awareness of their inner life.
   b. They do not suppress emotions, anxieties, and fantasies.
   c. They have self-understanding and become perceptive to their abilities and shortcomings.
   d. They are self-accepting—recognizing their abilities in a constructive manner.

2. Adaptability
   a. They are flexible. They can give up one idea to try another.
   b. They experiment. Experimentation is basic to all arts, which cannot help growing from one time period to the next.

3. Independence

a. They do not give in to peer values. Instead of "following the crowd," they look at other aspects of what is going on and do not bend to social pressures.

b. They are willing to take risks.

4. Respect

a. They learn to respect other artists for their individuality and contributions.

b. They have self-respect.

NUTRITION

If you want to produce the highest quality work possible, then you must have the will power to order and control your daily living. Because your body is the instrument of your work, you want to preserve your health so that it functions properly.

Eat regularly, without overindulging, and eat sensible foods that offer a nutritious and balanced diet. Avoid stimulants whenever possible, as they eventually tire and damage the body. Food faddism is dangerous for anyone, especially athletes. The training table of a skater ought to provide a balanced and sound diet. Some food fads give extremely restricted diets, so poorly balanced that chronic fatigue or even actual illness may result. Overeating can begin a vicious circle of overweight and fatigue. Instead, cultivate physical energy that is long lasting, with nutritious foods that have proper proportions of protein and vitamins.

When you start to run out of energy, do you reach automatically for "quick energy foods" like sugars and starches? They may give you the lift for the moment that you are looking for, but that soon wears out, and you find that you are more tired than you were before.

Also, consider that your brain is as much a physical mass of cells as other parts of your body. Therefore, when your body starts running out of fuel, it becomes more difficult to think, just as it does to move actively. When this happens, you begin to make errors in judgment. The body and mind must have the same type of fuel for energetic action. I highly recommend that you consult nutrition and sports medicine experts on the type

of training diet that your particular body needs.

STYLE

Style involves your attitude. To have style is to search continuously for something new and different. Being able to do something new with the same old steps and with the same body is inventing style.

No one is born with style. It is a learned process. If you have a great desire for it, and reach out for eloquent ways to express yourself, it will evolve into dynamic work, with fluidity and meaningful precision. This takes a lot of physical self-discipline and thinking from your superconscious mind. But it will result in a style that is not in any way like the style of anyone else, and not derivative of the way of moving of any teacher or artist under whom you study.

THE CREATIVE SPIRIT

Use the ways and methods in this book of creating original and interesting movements and patterns to unleash your creative spirit. You will intellectualize more as it develops. The exercises can become the structural framework for highly organized forms of expression. The knowledge and the tools learned here will not confine, limit, or make your art expression mechanized or regimented. On the contrary, they will make it possible for you to express more perfectly those things that are uniquely yours.

You cannot really be a great artist with only a part of you. You must involve your whole being with a passion. It is this passion that helps you to persevere, until you become the artist —a creator, a communicator, and, ultimately, an inspiration to others.

INDEX